EXPERTS & INFLUENCERS

THE LEADERSHIP EDITION

Rebecca Hall Gruyter, Compiler
#1 International Best Selling Author

RHG | MEDIA PRODUCTIONS™

Published 2019

Printed in the United States of America

Print ISBN: 978-1-7328885-2-4
Publisher Information:

RHG Media Productions

25495 Southwick Drive #103

Hayward, CA 94544

www.YourPurposeDrivenPractice.com

Acknowledgements

When writing an anthology, it takes many voices willing to join together to bring forth the book in a powerful and united way. It has been such an honor and privilege to work with this amazing group of Experts & Influencers. I want to thank these amazing leaders for entrusting us to bring forth and share their powerful stories.

I want to thank my husband for always cheering me on and encouraging me to SHINE! I thank God for giving me opportunities, opening doors, and bringing together the right people for this powerful project. I thank my parents for their love and support and my grandmothers for planting the legacy seeds to always choose to Bloom Where You Are Planted, Step Forward, and SHINE!

Contents

FOREWORD

"EXPERTS & INFLUENCERS SERIES: THE LEADERSHIP EDITION"
BY REBECCA HALL GRUYTER, BOOK COMPILER

Thank you for leaning into this powerful anthology! I'm honored and excited to bring this powerful book featuring over 18 experts that are committed to helping you **SHINE** powerfully in leadership! Our vision is to have our experts and influencers share insights, tips, tools, and wisdom in the area of leadership to support you powerfully on your leadership journey. We know leadership is not a solo journey and by coming together our goal is to help you step further into and more powerfully into your gifts, talents, and abilities as leaders. Together, as we lift each other up, we are all able to grow, reach more people, and have a greater impact than we do trying to do everything on our own.

In each chapter, our authors (all leadership experts and influencers) will equip and empower you to more fully step forward as a powerful leader. I believe this book is a living and interactive book that will speak wisdom, encouragement, and power into your life. I want to invite you to pause, take a deep breath, and be ready to receive these powerful chapters so they can ignite a fire in you, inspire courage in you, and focus to step fully into the leader that you are called to be.

We each need others to encourage us, to speak wisdom and truth to us, to love us and cheer us on, and to help us stand up again when we fall. This book will walk beside you to help you run and not grow weary, to complete all that you are called to complete, and to live on purpose and with great purpose while stepping more fully and powerfully into your calling of leadership.

In creating this book, I asked each leadership expert and influencer to share a chapter that includes their wisdom, tips, and insights to help you as a leader. We asked them to share what they wished they would have known about leadership, what they have learned, and their best tips and insights to support you on your leadership journey. Throughout the chapters you will feel a consistent and transparent heartbeat to support you in very real ways as the authors share authentically and powerfully from the heart. We want to make your journey easier for you to step forward and **SHINE**! As the book compiler, I'm so proud of what each co-author has shared in their chapters, and am honored to have each of them leaning in to support you. I am equally honored that you have said "yes" to our book and are entrusting us to support you on your journey.

Now it's your turn. Are you going to lean in and learn from the wisdom within this book? Will you let us walk beside you on your journey of life? We want to lift you up, support you, encourage, and empower you. It is your choice. You can choose to open the pages and let them pour into you, or you can put this book on a shelf. My heart and prayer are that you will say "yes" to you and lean into the powerful messages that are waiting to pour into you, your heart, and your life.

Here is how to get the most out of this powerful book. The book is divided into three sections, each one designed to meet you exactly where you are and to support you powerfully. **In the first section: Leadership and You,** our experts share everything from your relationship with leadership to answering your call to leadership. **In the second section: Your Leadership Toolbox,** our experts share how to tap into your gifts and talents in leadership to tools, tips, and inspiration to support you on your leadership journey. **In the third section: Your Leadership in Action,** our leaders share how to step fully into your leadership, bring in support for your leadership journey, and to take action and SHINE! At the end of each powerful chapter, you will find the author's bio and contact information. I encourage you to "friend" and follow those authors with whom you feel a powerful resonance and connection so that they can continue to pour into you and support you on your journey in life.

Special Augmented Reality Print Book Feature. We are excited to share we have added the powerful cutting-edge REVEALiO technology to the print version of our book. You can download the free app and then once it's uploaded on your smart device it will help the book cover and chapters come alive. After you download the free app onto your smart device, simply open the app and place the window over the cover of the book and a video message from us will start to play. Many of the authors in this book have also added a special video message to you too. So, make sure to open the app and use it in the beginning of each chapter (putting the picture and title of the author's chapter in the screen box) and those that have saved a video message for you will immediately start playing. Enjoy this special feature and personal messages from our powerful authors.

Now the next step is yours. Drink-in the insights, tips, and wisdom that are within these pages to serve, support, and inspire you. Take the time to pause, read, and reflect. Listen to the powerful messages of hope that are waiting for you within the pages of this book. It's not an accident that you purchased this book and are opening it to read. I invite you to lean in and truly receive the messages and wisdom that will speak to your heart and soul that you will find in these transformational and dynamic pages. Enjoy this rich collection of wisdom, insight, and encouragement being provided by our amazing Leadership Experts & Influencers. We can't wait to see you SHINE!

-----*Rebecca Hall Gruyter, Book Compiler*

Founder/Owner of Your Purpose Driven Practice and CEO of RHG Media Productions

Rebecca Hall Gruyter is an Influencer and Empowerment Leader committed to bringing Experts and Influencers forward so that together we can lean in and make the world a better place one heart and life at a time. She is the owner of *Your Purpose Driven Practice*, creator of the *Women's Empowerment Series* events/TV show, the *Speaker Talent Search™*, and *Your Success Formula™*. Rebecca is an in-demand speaker, an expert money coach, and a frequent guest expert on success panels, tele-summits, TV, and radio shows. Rebecca specializes in using her promotional reach of over 10 million to help you be seen, heard, and SHINE!

As the CEO of *RHG Media Productions™*, Rebecca launched the international TV Network (www.RHGTVNetwork.com) to bring even more positive and transformational programming to the world. In July 2017 she launched the Global RHG Magazine & TV Guide bringing inspirational influences to the world and their messages! In January 2018, she expanded RHG Publishing to now help individual authors bring their books forward as best sellers so they can be positioned as they bring their powerful book forward.

Rebecca is a popular and syndicated radio talk show host, #1 bestselling author (multiple times), and publisher who wants to help YOU impact the world powerfully!

(925) 787-1572
Rebecca@YourPurposeDrivenPractice.com
www.facebook.com/rhallgruyter (Facebook)
www.YourPurposeDrivenPractice.com (Main Website)
www.RHGTVNetwork.com (TV Network)
www.SpeakerTalentSearch.com (Free Opportunity for Speakers to get on More Stages)
www.EmpoweringWomenTransformingLives.com (Weekly Radio Show)
www.MeetWithRebecca.com (Calendar link to schedule a time to talk with Rebecca)

SECTION 1:

Leadership and You

THE BRIDGE TO BECOMING
A POWERFUL LEADER
BY ISAAC SAMUEL MILLER

How would you define leadership? Everyone has an opportunity to live their life in a way that's impactful and satisfying. But in order to truly be impactful we all must master the art of true leadership. In order to become a powerful leader you must travel along the only bridge that leads to success. As you continue to read this chapter in this timely book on leadership, you will begin to discover what bridge I'm referring to, and why this bridge is the only bridge to success.

Do You Know How To Become A Powerful Leader

A phenomenal leader is a true visionary! As a child my goal was to lead my vision into fruition. As a young boy I was acquiesced into poverty, and I use to think that selling drugs and depending on government assisted programs was my life's birthright. I have overcome overwhelming obstacles, and I have made it my mission in life to use my experienced strategy of winning in life to help leaders just like you to become not just a leader, but a powerful leader!

When I was 17 I became a self-employed fitness trainer while still enrolled in college as a full time student, and I have been a fitness trainer for over a decade. I have a degree in Therapeutic Recreation and Leisure Studies along with a minor in Physical Education. I'm a Certified Strength & Conditioning Specialist and a Certified Therapeutic Recreation Specialist. My work experience consists of managing personal training sales teams, developing and implementing intervention strategies for patients with physical, mental, emotional, and social ailments. Furthermore, I help various businesses to improve their sales and business strategies by examining their companies' processes along with the execution of their processes. I'm a motivational speaker and an author of a self-help book entitled, **Just Get Up: And Manifest Your Inner Genius**. Finally, I live by two of my own original quotes which are: **"Don't let one stop in your life represent an eternity of No's"** and **"You must give great something to look up to!"**

Throughout the course of my entrepreneurial years I have learned how to become an impactful leader, while maintaining my resolve to pull the visions of my life that I dreamed of out of my head and into reality. As a child, I often contemplated suicide while battling the overwhelming temptation to live a debased life. When I was a kid I desperately sought out various ways of making money. I hated growing up poor and I hated the thought of being brought up through government assisted programs. During my childhood my dad was a drug user and he was absent in my life, and my mom was sick and incapable of working because she is a paranoid schizophrenia. I was able to cope and fight my way out of poverty as a child, because I took a stand to focus on developing a relationship with Jehovah God. I asked God for wisdom to show me how to use my gifts, and I asked him to help me discover my purpose in life, and of course, He delivered! I'm excited to share with you the wisdom that I have unearthed through the power of true faith and self-belief.

<u>Why The World Needs You To Become A Powerful Leader</u>

Before I begin to share with you the keys for becoming a powerful leader, it's necessary to refresh your memory regarding the importance of being an effective leader. As you continue to read, you will begin to learn how to use the proper tools to tap into a part of your leadership abilities that will make you a great leader. Also, it's important to mention that if we all wholeheartedly devote ourselves to learning how to properly exercise our minds, then eventually we will train our way into discovering our unique purposes in life. All of the billions of people on our planet are capable of being a living example of success. But in order to become a living example of success all of us must learn how to be a leader! Discovering the true meaning of success is a pressing issue in the world today, because we live in a world where dreams are buried while still being alive. The world is governed by sincere strides for success that are often diligently implemented in error. This error is born whenever people mistakenly believe they aren't capable of living a righteous, meaningful, passionate, and successful life.

This error can be compared to doing an exercise wrong for many years and the exercise method doesn't produce the intended results. In fact, implementing an exercise for a plethora of years with improper form will inevitably lead to an injury, which often incapacitates one's capabilities to progress to success. Unfortunately, millions of people choose to improperly exercise their minds, which has produced mental injuries that have resulted in untimely deaths, increases in poverty, unsatisfying lives, depression, crimes, and the painful experiences of never unleashing the unstoppable leader that exists in all of us!

The truth is, we all are seeking success, but there are so many misguided guides in the world and sincere people are often led astray. The fact that you are reading this book is an indication that you're among the few who realizes their potential. More than likely you want to help end the world's misguidance or fight your way into implementing the proper plan for your personal success. Here is my promise to you: if you travel along the only bridge that leads to becoming a powerful leader, then not only will you become unstoppable, but you will be equipped to help millions of sincere people who are desperately seeking success. However, you may be wondering what is the only bridge that leads to becoming an unstoppable leader?

How To Become A Powerful Leader

Throughout my journey of maintaining my self-employment status I was faced with several adversities that tested my willpower and my steadfastness toward working for myself. After I graduated from college I was faced with several opportunities to work for someone else. I went on a lot of job interviews because people were constantly in my ear telling me that I needed to abandon my solo career in personal training. My mom and trusted friends told me that I wouldn't be able to provide for myself or a family, and they repeatedly mentioned there wasn't security in personal training. All I heard was, " What if you lose all of your clients and what about health insurance?" Unfortunately, those negative insights produced unnecessary fears within my belief system, which compelled me to go on six different job interviews over the course of a three-year period during and after college.

I received five job offers from lucrative companies that had guaranteed a plethora of benefits. However, there was something within me that forced me to turn down each and every job offer. Eventually, I began to realize that everyone who was offering their unsolicited advice had my best interests at heart, but they were misguided in what was right for my gifts and path. I began to realize the incontrovertible truth that the people who were attempting to give me advice, never worked for themselves or pursued the career path that I was pursuing. So, I began to ask myself, "How can my mother give me advice on personal training when she has never been a trainer?" I realized that my mom didn't know anyone who was successful as a fitness trainer and she knew very little about the fitness industry.

In the preceding paragraph I purposefully stated: "She didn't know anyone who was a successful personal trainer." **I've learned never to focus on the people who have failed at an endeavor you want to pursue but to focus on the people who are winning in the pursuits that you want to pursue.** This concept provides proof that if you can find one person who has done or is doing exactly what you desire to do, then you can do it too! So, even if only one person throughout the history of mankind has been successful at what you're passionate about then that's enough proof. You don't need three or three million people to validate your life's pursuits.

Here are some things you do need: self-belief, humility, flexibility, constant refinement of your abilities, honesty with yourself, several great strategies, great support systems, knowledge, obsession with greatness, a no quit mentality, insane amounts of effort, a clear understanding of your gifts and exactly how to use your gifts to solve problems, immediate action, knowing exactly how to make yourself valuable, and full reliance on God. Once I fully committed myself to those constructs I became unstoppable and I said to myself, "I will work for myself for the rest of my life." I am Isaac the motivational speaker, I am Isaac the fitness trainer, I am Isaac the author, I am Isaac the minister, and I am Inspiration. The first two steps to becoming a powerful leader are: to truly believe in yourself and to know who you truly are. Who are you?

A Powerful Leader Must Believe
Wholeheartedly In Their Potential

The most important thing that you must work on every day is your belief system about yourself. Why is this so important? It's simple; if you don't believe in yourself and your ideas then no one else will. If you aren't truly inspired from within, you won't be an effective leader. An effective leader is a go-getter and someone who is willing to question established ways of doing things. Most importantly, there is a difference between universal laws and rules that possess fallacy, so be alert and aware of the differences, but always be willing to question and form your own unique path.

A true leader must be self-motivated and emotionally brave. Being emotionally brave is another meaning for courage and courage as a leader will often mean doing things that no one else understands. As a leader you can never submit to an inferior approach that lacks substance. Yes, you should be humble and adaptable, but don't negate your dreams because other people don't share your vision.

The bridge to success is developing an obsession with self-development and recognizing that life's possibilities are unlimited. **Your body may have limitations, but your mind doesn't. Never place limits on your mind and always question the impossible.** If you objectively review every single thing that exists on our planet, you will realize the indisputable truth that everything starts with an idea. **Remember this: always promote your ideas and form a plan of action to bring your ideas into fruition. Adapt this as your motto: lead your ideas forward and into reality.** A leader must develop experience through trial and error. You must seek failure so that success will seek you through your failures; however, you will only see the truth in what I'm saying if you never give up on working on getting better every single day!

A leader must understand his or herself and you must develop unmatched wisdom about your area of expertise. You develop wisdom by studying and taking in knowledge every single day regarding the subject matter you want to master. After you take in knowledge you must apply the new things you're learning immediately in each domain of your business settings. Through repetition you will begin to develop understanding regarding what works and what doesn't work. If you relentlessly invest in your mind every day by listening to audio programs, reading, dreaming, reviewing your goals, talking to other powerful leaders, praying to God, and positively nurturing your subconscious mind you will be unstoppable.

You must develop a clear vision of who you are and what direction you want your business and life to go. For a second, imagine following three different GPSes with three different directions all at the same time. Do you think you would ever arrive at your desired location if you followed three different GPSes with three different locations all at the same time?

The Art of Narrowing Your Focus

You must have a clear vision and a good precise method on how to get there. Sometimes having a precise method means to narrow your focus to one thing at a time. The only time an effective leader tackles several tasks all at once is when the tasks are interconnected. You won't always know how to achieve your goals when you first attempt to travel to them, but you must know what your goals are. Some people never become good leaders because they train people and themselves to throw darts at targets that haven't been clearly identified. So know your goals, learn how to travel to your goals, and learn how to succinctly narrow your focus.

Compare narrowing your focus to a mechanic who is managing their time as they're repairing their car. Suppose a mechanic named John has two flat tires and he needs two new tires, an oil change in 800 miles, windshield wiper fluid, and gas. Furthermore, suppose John decides to fix his car during his hour lunch break at 12 because he has to travel somewhere after his lunch break. John only has an hour to work on these repairs because his lunch break is an hour. Based on John's experience he estimates that it will take him an hour and 30 minutes to fix all of the repairs. However, if John fixes everything then it will make him late for his destination right after his lunch break.

Would it be wise for John to drive to purchase windshield wiper fluid and do an oil change that can wait a few more weeks? The only things that are necessary for John at the moment are gas and getting his tires repaired. Similarly, you must learn how to manage your tasks, prioritize, and teach others to do the same. If you master the ability to narrow your focus, then the people you influence will learn from your example how to be more productive as they're implementing the art of narrowing their focuses as well.

My challenge to you is to learn how to manage yourself and start a self-improvement program that will force you to become a hard worker. Once you develop a true love for the fact that you can improve every day then you're officially traveling the only bridge that will lead to you becoming a powerful leader. In conclusion, you must remember this as well: you are a genius and you can do all things with God's guidance."

Tips To Becoming A Powerful Leader

1. Believe wholeheartedly in your potential.
2. Narrow your focus.
3. Take action!

Isaac Miller

My name is Isaac Miller and I was born on July 19, 1988. I'm an entrepreneur and I've worked for myself as a full-time personal trainer for 13 years. I'm also a minister, motivational speaker, and an author. My motto is: if you don't believe it will happen for a certainty then why waste your time pursuing it! I grew up in two very impoverished neighborhoods in Baton Rouge, LA, and those neighborhoods are called Zion City and Boot Town. Furthermore, I was a fatherless boy who was fortunate to escape the gripping jaws of drugs and poverty. My path to success was full of adversities, and I struggled to achieve my dreams because I lacked the proper support and no one believed in me.

When I turned 11, I made it my mission in life to make something out of myself and to expose my gifts to the world. I always felt special as a young boy, but I struggled to believe in myself because of my broken atmosphere that lacked parental guidance. In my desperation to find a way from no way at all I embarked upon a journey of self-discovery that culminated in me becoming an entrepreneur at 17 years of age.

I have a degree in Therapeutic Recreation and Leisure Studies and a minor in Physical Education. I've been fortunate to train well over 1,000 people and I've consistently worked with a majority of these people for over a decade. I'm also a life coach and I engage in a full-time preaching work to help people to establish a closer relationship with God.

Isaacfittherapy@gmail.com
225-397-2704
www.JustGetUpWithIsaac.com
Facebook: justgetupwithisaac
LinkedIn: justgetupwithisaac
Instagram: justgetupwithisaac
Twitter: justgetupwithisaac
Pinterest: justgetupwithisaac
Youtube: Isaac Miller spoken word performances:
"Self-belief" and "The Homeless Equation"

LEVELING UP – A BUSINESS LEADER'S JOURNEY TO SUCCESS
BY MICHELLE CALLOWAY

I love it when I'm in the zone. Thoughts are flowing freely, my mind is sharp, I'm saying and doing all of the right things. It's a euphoric feeling of invincibility... I'm crushing this!

So, what is "the zone" and how do we get in it? The zone is that proverbial place where focus and execution produce a higher level of performance and progress than average. We can only get in the zone through much practice and focus.

> *"There are no secrets to success. It is the result of preparation, hard work, and learning from failure." - Colin Powell*

Building a business and becoming a thought leader in your industry is no easy feat. It takes a lot of hard work and focus. When I answered the call to start an augmented reality technology business to positively impact people's relationships, I didn't have a clue where to begin. It is a journey of personal and professional growth that comes in stages, or zones. Your influence increases as you level up from one zone to the next.

The Prep Zone

"Unless you have a definite, precise, clearly set goal, you are not going to realize the maximum potential that lies within you." - Zig Ziglar

All good businesses start with an idea. That's just the beginning though. **Once you determine who your competition is in that space, you need to determine what your unique identifier will be—that "thing" that will set you apart from the rest.** Hopefully it will be something that no one else can replicate.

When my husband and I began going through the planning phase of our new business it quickly became apparent how much work there was to do. We had to study the landscape, the opportunity, the competition, the cost.

I realized the "cost" was going to be more than monetary. Creating this business was going to require time, energy, resources, sacrifice, and possibly relocating away from our home town, away from family, to better position ourselves for success. Was I up for it? Were we up for it? Was our marriage up for it? We asked those tough questions, and we both answered a resounding, "YES!"

We set out to write our plan, so we could get our funding and get underway building our new business. I struggled with this planning part of the process the most. I am an action-taker and I wanted to get straight to the fun part, making sales. I had already built a prototype at this point, so I had a proof of concept, which is very helpful in the technology world. But there was a lot of foundational work still to be done and many details that needed addressing along the way.

The Construction Zone

"Great things in business are never done by one person. They're done by a team of people." - Steve Jobs

I had the wonderful opportunity to work on a friend's ranch every summer from when I was age 11 to when I was 16 years old. The ranch taught me that it doesn't matter if you don't feel like doing the work, it has to be done. No one will do it for you. You don't get to call in sick. You work until the work is done.

From this experience, I learned perseverance, determination, and grit. These characteristics propel me forward through adversity and unexpected barriers. When it comes to bringing people on to my team, I expect them to adopt these same characteristics. Being an entrepreneur can be emotionally taxing. I need a team that I can depend on in the best of times and in the worst of times.

Bring on team leaders. It's great to hire someone that does their job well, but it's even better if you hire someone that will take on a leadership position within that division. Ultimately, you need to be free to focus on fulfilling the company's bigger vision not leading the many divisions within your organization.

Be selective on who you bring into your company culture. Each one of your initial team members is a pillar in your organizational structure. Will they stand the test of time? Can you see them growing along with you and your company well into the future? Do they get along well with others? Look for early signs and fire and replace quickly until you have the team you want moving forward.

As a team, begin implementing your plan. Each team member doing their part to benefit the whole. When you're ready, test it, get feedback, and make appropriate modifications. Try again. It's a process. In order for your idea to blossom into something sustainable, it needs to be developed, nurtured, and fortified.

There is something so inherently satisfying about the feeling you get when you see the fruits of your own labor. I encourage my team to take pride in working hard. Pride in building something that will give them a great sense of satisfaction when they see it finished.

The Loading Zone

"A mentor is someone who sees more talent and ability within you than you see in yourself, and helps bring it out of you." - Bob Proctor

Working on a ranch is hard work, but it's simple work for the most part. **Building a business is not simple, and I quickly realized how important mentors and advisors are.** My husband and I discovered that we were outside of our knowledgebase in many areas when we began the planning process of our business.

We needed knowledge and mentoring, and we needed it quick. Have you ever had so much knowledge thrown at you that it felt like you were drinking from a firehose? That's the way I felt after I joined an incubator for startups in Berkeley, CA. Evidently, planning out your business was only part of the hard work. Figuring out how to implement each part of the plan was another. We had an advisor for every aspect of running our business, and I was uploading valuable information as fast as I could.

If you want to build a quilt, find a quiltmaker who's craftsmanship you admire, and ask them questions. How did they get started quilting? Who taught them to quilt? How much money did they need to start their quilting business? What are three valuable things they learned about quilting or the quilting business that the wish they'd known before they started? The answers to these questions will help you greatly if you want to be a successful quilter.

Find out where your mentors hang out with other industry experts. Do they have a networking group you can join? Ask if you can take a few of them out to lunch. Glean as much as you can from those in your industry that are crushing it.

The Friend Zone

*"A true friend is one who overlooks your failures
and tolerates your success!" - Doug Larson*

Good friends are worth their weight in gold. A good friend knows you inside and out and will do anything to help you when you're in need. They love you enough to tell you what you need to hear rather than be silent and watch you career off a cliff.

My journey as a business leader requires a solid support system. The more popular you become, the more naysayers you will have. I have had to develop very thick skin. It takes 10 positive comments to balance out one negative comment in your psyche.

Surround yourself with people who encourage you and build you up because they believe in you and what you are doing. Don't be surprised when you find that some of your "friends" aren't as supportive as you would've hoped they would be.

When you become an industry expert or a thought leader, it changes your life, and the lives of those around you. The amount of knowledge you gain through studying and refining your expertise will forever change the way you think and see the world.

Sometimes the people closest to you don't like the new way you look at things. They cry out and pull on your heartstrings to keep you in their zone. Much like the story of the crabs in a pot over low heat. The other crabs will pull the one crab trying to climb out back into the pot and eventually they all perish as the water continues to heat up.

I have had to make some tough decisions on who I will allow into my inner sacred circle. I've cried over losing friends. I'm on a path to fulfill a higher purpose for my life and I have to honor that and be true to myself. The quality of the friends I have around me now is so amazing! They are so full of light, hope, and adventure; it's refreshing. **I don't look back on what I've lost, I choose to focus on what I've gained.**

Purging unhealthy or toxic relationships from our lives is paramount to the growth process. Doing so can be incredibly difficult, but it can also be the most liberating thing you will ever do in your life. Reach out to a supportive friend to help you through the process. You don't have to do this alone. Lean on your true friends.

The Impact Zone

"EQ is . . . the strongest driver of leadership and personal excellence." – Travis Bradberry, author of Emotional Intelligence 2.0

Do you have someone in your life that you look up to? Do you read books from specific industry leaders to inspire you and guide you? What is it about that person that attracts you to them? What is it that they are doing well that you can emulate?

"Be the Leader You Would Follow Voluntarily,
Without Title or Position." – Brian Tracy

I try to lead by example. My parents taught me to make a name for myself because my reputation is my foundation in life. **Your reputation will be what warrants your success as a business owner, a thought leader, and an influencer. Are you the "real deal?"**

Below is a list of things that you can do to build your reputation and increase your level of impact and influence:

- Be confident
- Be authentic
- Be vulnerable at times
- Ask for input
- Honor your word
- Be kind
- Be truthful
- Dress for success
- Speak from a stage
- Author a book
- Publish expertise articles
- Build a community
- Interview other experts
- Announce accomplishments
- Share wisdom through live broadcast or video
- Share inspirational quotes on social media

The End Zone

"Education is the catalyst that will hone and sharpen our talents,
skills, and abilities and cause them to blossom". - Joseph B. Wirthlin

Once you obtain the recognition of being a thought leader and industry expert, it requires effort to maintain that reputation. It's like maintaining your weight after losing 100 lbs. You need to develop a maintenance plan or you may quickly find yourself backsliding.

I have a daily regime of reading and learning from others in my industry and from those that inspire me. I always tell myself, "If you're not learning, you're dying." I then share what I've learned with my followers on a regular basis through live broadcasts, blog posts, or newsletter e-blasts.

Try to remain humble no matter how popular you become. Staying humble is good for your success as it makes you more relatable, and it is good for your soul as you treat others with dignity and respect. Treating others well will always come back to reward you, plus it's the right thing to do.

Lastly, I would recommend that you don't get comfortable. When we become comfortable it leads to complacency. Great leaders don't come from a place of complacency. Leaders are made when they step outside of their comfort zone. Be willing to step out of your comfort zone!

Key Steps for Your Leadership Success!

1. Prep and plan
2. Build your team
3. Find the right mentors
4. Discover who are truly your friends
5. Build, manage, and mind your reputation
6. Step out of your comfort zone!
7. Be willing to lead and SHINE!

Michelle Calloway

Michelle Calloway is the Founder and CEO of REVEALiO, Inc., an innovative software development company specializing in augmented reality video marketing technology. She is driven to success in response to a calling she believes has been placed on her life. Her goal is to make augmented reality experiences accessible and affordable for everyone, to enhance human relationships, and empower business owners to have more impact, influence, and income.

Recently featured in Inc. Magazine, Michelle combines her expertise in visual communication with the emerging world of augmented reality (AR). This interactive technology overlays virtual content on top of real-world objects when they are viewed through a mobile or wearable smart device.

Her mission is to empower small businesses to gain the ultimate competitive advantage by captivating their audiences and influencing their buying decisions.

Her vision of REVEALiO became clear when she witnessed the powerful heartfelt connection that took place when a deployed U.S. soldier received a REVEALiO greeting card from his girlfriend. When the card "came alive" with her talking to him on the card, it rocked him to his core. He folded it up and carried it with him every day because it made him feel as if she was right there with him. This powerful human response is what inspired Michelle Calloway to develop and launch REVEALiO – Cards That Come Alive!

Michelle wants to share her inspirational story and teach the power of augmented reality as a marketing tool to entrepreneurs, small business owners, CEOs, video professionals, and publishers. Her heart is to empower small businesses to gain the ultimate competitive advantage by captivating their audiences and influencing their buying decisions.

Email: mcalloway@revealio.com
Phone: 415-870-7894
Personal Website: https://michellecalloway.us
Business Website: https://www.revealio.com
Personal Facebook: https://www.facebook.com/michelle.callowaybowden
Business Facebook: https://business.facebook.com/revealio
LinkedIn: https://www.linkedin.com/in/michelle-calloway-revealio
Twitter: https://twitter.com/Smileyshell69
Instagram: https://www.instagram.com/micalloway
YouTube: https://www.youtube.com/channel/UC4LzcwGHM1IJjmLHGRtnJLA

HELPING TEENS STEP
INTO THEIR LEADERSHIP POWER
BY KIMBERLY SCHEHRER, MA

Teens are our future. They are the leaders of tomorrow, which is why we need to support them in being the best versions of themselves today–*and I'd love to lock arms with you in making it happen.*

Why? Because it is one thing to expect that teens will take the weight of the world and lead the future, and it's entirely different to have them actually feel confident and prepared to be the leaders we know they're capable of.

Having coached teens to be better students for over a decade, I can tell you that many teens feel like *the world is sending them mixed messages.* On the one hand, if they want to get into college, everyone seems to be saying they "should" step up as leaders, but on a day-to-day basis, they feel more like the world wants them to be followers:

- They're following what their parents tell them to do (or they'll suffer consequences)
- They're following what their teachers tell them to do (or they'll suffer consequences)

- And extremely sadly, they're following the belief that if they're struggling in school today, they won't have much of a future anyway, so what's the point?

So, how do we stop sending our "future leaders" mixed messages and truly help our teens step into their leadership power? It takes a village of adults in their lives, who are on the same page about best leadership practices and are committed to teens' success, especially when our teens are doubting themselves.

Nothing Speaks Louder Than Your Role Modeling

You are a role model. Your words are impactful, but your actions are seen and heard more loudly and clearly than any words. So, be mindful of your actions.

Take a minute and contemplate how are you being a role model of leadership yourself. Where are you truly stepping into your leadership power and where are you stepping back and/or feeling like a follower?

From our first memory, we are making conscious and unconscious choices for ourselves. But we may not consider ourselves leadership material. It's time to dispel that myth. You are a leader of one very important individual. Your influence and impact determine the destiny of one cherished soul. Yes, that unique person is YOU!

"Whether you think you can, or can't," said Henry Ford, "either way, you are right."

Being real with ourselves helps us better relate to what our teens are going through.

Have Compassion: It's Hard to Step Up When Your Self-Esteem Is Down

As we all know, grades are just one of many predictors of teens' ultimate success in life. However, because of how much grades are played up (especially by authority figures), teens may feel like grades really are everything, and if they're not doing well, they'll never be "smart enough" to turn the situation around.

Let's take a teen who is struggling in school and pretty much feels stupid. The ongoing struggles can and often crushes their confidence and self-esteem. It's hard to get that back. Let's face it, when you don't have the confidence, you are also filtering future experiences in a more negative light. Many of us tend to align with our own negative self-judgment rather than to see possibilities or opportunities. Our momentum and hopes for progress are stifled.

Be Open to Their Vision

I personally relate to the struggling teens I coach. I was that high school student who really didn't apply myself or really believe in myself that I could do much better than B's or C's in some of the difficult subjects for me. I also hung around peers who were not applying themselves. But when I got into college, I had my vision.

At the time, I wanted to be a clinical psychologist and needed a graduate degree to do that. I was very clear in my vision. Since graduate school is highly competitive, I needed to improve my grades and take my academics more seriously. My vision gave me focus, clarity, purpose, and motivation. It ultimately led to me accomplishing my goals. I graduated with honors from college and graduated with honors from graduate school.

If you looked at me in high school, you would not have imagined that would happen. I think part of leadership is being aware of your knowing and trusting to do what works for YOU despite naysayers, even if it's your well-meaning parents, well-meaning friends, or colleagues.

Help Teens Define Their Values

One of the most important ways you can support teens is by helping them define their values, which is an important aspect of leadership. Values define your operating system.

This world judges us and we judge ourselves. **When you know what you stand for, what your values are, it allows you to not align with judgments and instead, align with who you are regardless of what the world says.** Your values are one component for creating the life that you desire. Give yourself permission to stand strong in your values even when others disagree with you.

When I was in college and doing well in psychology, I had to pick a minor. I chose biology and it took me three times to attempt the completion of the first science course because I didn't believe that I was smart enough for the labs and Latin words. My father said that if I dropped the class, I'd never go back to it and wouldn't graduate college. Instead, I listened to my own inner guidance and chose to withdraw from the class. I took the class the following semester, and I excelled. It served me to hear the advice and step forward after checking in with my values and truth.

Don't Be Afraid to Ask Yourself: Does This Work for Me?

A lot of times we go through the motions based on what other people expect or their opinions on how to do something, and we end up not being aligned with who we are. We do it, and it just doesn't work for us.

Instead of going through all of that, acknowledge what works for you and what doesn't and those are your boundaries. Setting boundaries for yourself is important to staying congruent with your integrity and serves as inspiration to others when you are interacting with them.

Where do you need to set more boundaries in your life in general? Where do you need to set more boundaries when interacting with teens? Boundary-setting is also a great way to be a role model of leadership.

Discover Passions and Play to Strengths

Teens can often be passionate, but sometimes it isn't clear what their specific passion is.

To aid you in discovering your passion, think back to what you enjoyed doing as a child. How did you play? That can give you clues and help you pinpoint where your passion lies today. Your passion will call upon your strengths and gifts. **Playing to your strengths is a mark of a leader.**

As a child, I loved to play school and being the teacher. Education and teens are very important to me and this is why I founded the Academy for Independence. I'm passionate about teens because it took me so many years to look at my limiting beliefs and how I was sabotaging myself. I eventually realized what I needed to do to fully live the way I wanted to. I enjoy working with teens so they don't have to spend 20 or more years stifling their dreams or cutting off pieces of themselves to fit into someone else's mold. I want them to have the confidence to blaze their own trail so that they can live a more fulfilled and passionate life.

Many of us are told to improve our weaknesses, but we rarely get the message to play to our strengths. Teamwork is an important part of leadership. If you are aware of your own strengths and see how you can apply them in leadership, then I feel that gives you greater awareness and openness to seeing other people's strengths. When you work as a team, all of you can be working to your strengths and leveraging those strengths. Playing to each other's strengths creates an outcome that has more impact and a more positive result.

Wake Up to Gratitude

Leaders understand the importance of gratitude. Take this opportunity to go beyond the obvious of health, home, or happiness. In keeping with the theme of leadership beginning with you, every morning write down three things you are grateful for about YOU. Your gratitude may be about what you have accomplished, or acknowledgement of your strengths or personality traits. Doing this every day helps set the stage for you to be aware of your gifts as your day unfolds and how you are making a difference in the world by sharing your gifts.

It's also fun and I encourage to share what you're grateful for with your teen so they see how gratitude is making a difference in your life and may follow your example.

Say: Goodbye Comfort, Hello Better Grades!

When I take on a challenge that is something out of my comfort zone, I remind myself that this is my chance to be bold. I make up my mind that I'll take a risk. I'm going to try it. If it doesn't work out that's ok, I can make another choice. That's the thing about failure and things not working out; it's one way you learn. You'll learn something from each choice which will help contribute to you making a more congruent choice later. So, if I choose something and it didn't work for me then later, whatever I gleaned from it not working out, I can use that lesson to help me make a different and better choice next time.

Recently, I was working with a college student who said, "I'm not a good student." He'd been pulled out of schools and changed high schools often because he wasn't doing well. When I started working with him, he was struggling in college. By the end of the quarter, he got a 4.0. His first 4.0 ever! I asked him if he believed he was a good student now.

"Yeah," he replied. "I have what it takes."

He turned it around. He had a vision. He had an end goal of a career and earning some money to be able to live the life he desires. Now he's chosen a major, and he's got a vision and the motivation to make that vision come true. When he was a "bad student," he attracted friends who also didn't take school seriously and who received poor grades. Now when he started putting forth his best effort, he was risking his relationship with his peers. He was getting a little scared that his friends would leave as he became more serious about his goals for himself. Sometimes that does happen, which can hold us back because we don't want to lose our friends.

Nevertheless, he took a bold step. He put himself first, which is leadership. He's role modeling for those friends that they can change their act around too and get serious about school or they could leave and not be his friends. Either way, he's going forward to make his dreams come true. And it's an example of not fitting in, perhaps outgrowing his friends, and risking his community of peers. He'll get different peers now who will support where he is at. But in that transition period, it's not so comfortable. He's choosing for himself. He also realized that he had to make changes in his environment to foster better learning and living habits.

Let's Lock Arms to Support Teens' Success

Teens today are our next generation of leaders, so it's crucial that they be confident and have their passion for change in the world. It's important to support them with that.

So often in life we think it's about right or wrong. You want to get the right answer. You want to make the right choice. You want to do the right thing. Sometimes, we get caught in the trap of searching for the right answer, and not getting anything wrong, that we forget to trust ourselves. In truth, the more we develop our own awareness and inner knowing of what we love to do, our strengths, and what works for us, the more likely we are to hold high self-esteem and succeed at creating our reality according to our dreams.

One way we can support our youth, and develop greater awareness and trust within ourselves, is by coming together in a community to share best practices, inspiration, and our struggles. I invite you to join our Facebook community of parents titled, *Parents Empowering Teens to Achieve Their Dreams!* (The link is posted at the end of my chapter.) This is a community of parents who have a safe place to talk about their struggles and WINS with teens all year so we move from isolation to a global community of support and trust.

<u>Here is a review of the tips we discussed to achieve leadership:</u>

- **Nothing Speaks Louder Than Your Role Modeling for Teens** – Be mindful of your actions.
- **Have Compassion: It's Hard to Step Up When Your Self-Esteem Is Down** – Listen to your teen's struggles and acknowledge that a bad choice, or poor grades, are not permanent. We can change things around and choose a different course.
- **Be Open to Your Teen's Vision** – Their vision will motivate them to take action for better results.
- **Help Teens Define Their Values** – Clarity of values promotes teens to align with integrity and let go of others' judgments of them.
- **Don't Be Afraid to Ask Yourself: Does This Work for Me?** – Acknowledge boundaries for yourself and others.

- **Discover Passions and Play to Strengths** – Ask your teen, how did you play as a child? Where does that passion show up in your life today?
- **Wake Up to Gratitude** – Begin each day writing down three gratitudes about yourself.
- **Say: Goodbye Comfort, Hello Better Grades!** – Step out of your comfort zone, be bold, and take a risk.

Kimberly Schehrer

Kimberly Schehrer is a Teen Breakthrough Expert and Founder of Academy for Independence. She specializes in leadership, education, and personal development. She works closely with teens who she feels are a misunderstood group brimming with potential. Kimberly has an MA in Counseling Psychology and has over a decade's experience working with parents and teens as a Teen Breakthrough Expert, counselor, and an education specialist at schools, private institutions, and within the community in Silicon Valley and beyond.

Closed FB Group-Parents Empowering Teens to Achieve Their Dreams! https://bit.ly/2Rq8LpW

LinkedIn: https://www.linkedin.com/in/teen-breakthrough-expert/
Twitter Link: https://twitter.com/AFI_LifeCoaches
Website: AFI4ME.com/ **Cell:** 831.239.2788/
Email: kimberly@afi4me.com

LIVE A LIFE YOU WANT TO LEAD
BY STEFFAN SURDEK

Courage is one of those interesting words people like to talk about. Some people equate courage with fearlessness; I think it ties in better with bravery. Courage is not about being fearless in life; it is being able to acknowledge your fears and overcome them.

We sometimes seem to forget our lives reflect the various choices we make every single day. How do we choose to look at various situations in our lives? Which conversations do we choose to have or not to have with others? What do we choose to tolerate or experience in our daily lives? Making some of these choices requires more courage from us than others.

Courage often comes with a willingness to take responsibility for our lives. It is easy to blame others for what is going on in our lives. It takes courage to recognize there is one constant in everything we do and face: ourselves!

Living the life you want to lead is a very personal topic for me. For years professionally, I was able to step into leadership and my employers and colleagues valued me for it. Imagine my surprise when one day, I changed jobs and suddenly, all this was no longer true. For a bit more than year, I worked in a company where my managers ignored and snuffed my leadership skills. It turned me into a dormant leader for the first time in my career.

During the short time I was there, it felt like people were trying to make me forget I had leadership abilities. It occurred to me as if they wanted me to fall asleep and conform to my working environment. They did not want me to be the leader that I had the potential to be.

I often refer to that year as the worst in my professional career, but it forced me to take a closer look at myself. What was my leadership based on and how was I giving that experience to the people around me? Thinking back on it now, it was one of those crucial moments in my life that forced me to change and grow as a person.

The prison you create for yourself

When things get hard in our lives, our own beliefs can create a prison for ourselves without us even realizing it. Our limiting beliefs can form these invisible walls around us that constrain us. One day, as I took a closer look at myself during that difficult professional year, I had an epiphany of sorts—I realized that I had a choice. I could either:

1. Fall asleep and conform like others around me did. There was nothing wrong with doing that. I could have stayed in that company a long time if I did.
2. Remember who I was and who I wanted to be and step into it. If the environment did not want that, then another employer surely would.

Since then, I seek out dormant leaders in organizations where I am coaching and I help them awaken their leadership everywhere in their life. We have the potential to be leaders everywhere in our lives not just at work; we just need to choose to step into our leadership.

As a coach, when I find dormant leaders, I often ask them why they choose to stay in their current situations if they are so unhappy. Here are some of the recurring answers I hear from them:

*   It is the same everywhere anyways, I'd rather stay with the devil I know.
*   I come here for the paycheck. We all need to make money, right?
*   Is it possible to be happy at work? I have never been happy anywhere anyway.
*   Why should I speak up for myself, what is it going to change? No one is going to listen.

These statements can point to many different things. Do you have the courage or skills to speak up for yourself with your boss or to make the choice to look for a different job? Could it be that sometimes you hide your lack of courage by settling or enduring a situation you do not want?

When I went through a one-year coaching course, I had a big personal breakthrough moment. I was speaking to a fellow participant about a difficult situation I was going through at the time.

At one point, I was sharing with him "the rules" that were blocking me from resolving it. He asked me some questions and challenged my beliefs. **Through his questions, I came to realize I was following a set of rules that I had created by myself.** Without realizing it, I created my own little prison cell that I lived in for many years.

It was a really powerful moment for me. Visually, it was as if the world around me faded away and I started seeing myself in a prison cell instead. **When I looked around, I noticed the door to the cell was wide open all the time, but I could never see it for myself.** I was too busy following the rules and doing stuff to keep busy. In a moment, I went from feeling powerless to feeling powerful instead. I no longer needed to hold back, because I could choose to step out of the prison my beliefs had created in my life.

Have you ever considered why you keep dwelling about your current situation? Why are you not making any changes? What prison cell did you create for yourself?

Choose how you view your life

When we get stuck as dormant leaders, the biggest thing we do is use the law of attraction against ourselves. We see the world as negative and disempowering so we filter whatever happens around us through that lens. Then the negativity we believe becomes a self-fulfilling prophecy.

As people, one of our greatest superpowers we have is our ability to choose how we perceive a situation. It is like a filter that we can decide to apply to what is being said or to what is happening.

For example, **when someone tells you something negative you have a choice**. We can apply one of the following filters:

- This person hates me and wants to insult me or make me mad.
- This person is trying to say something important to them but may be awkward expressing it.
- Wow, where is that from? Tell me more?

Depending on the filter that you choose to apply, your reaction to it will be very different. It is not important if the filter you choose represents reality or not. What matters is the space that it creates for you to choose a different way to respond.

In my dormant leader experience, I chose to see my leaders as being new to their roles and awkward at it. I also consciously chose to be more open and help them instead of grumbling and being miserable. It created space for me to create new opportunities to help them. Instead of blaming them and being angry, I turned it into something healthier for myself and for them.

Choosing how life occurs to you allows you to create a different reality that can be a lot more empowering. It allows you to see the world from a different perspective. This will attract different things in your life than what you are experiencing now.

Step into your courage

If you are frustrated and/or feel stuck or trapped, have you ever considered why you keep dwelling about your current situation? Why are you not making any changes? Sometimes we blame others because it is easier than looking at our own limitations.

For example, you may be afraid and not have the courage to have a difficult conversation with your boss or your team or client. It could be because you feel you have trouble expressing yourself? Or maybe you feel you lack the skills to have the conversation you want to have? What are you doing to address this?

Take a look at the people around you in your life. Who do you know that has the skills you are looking for? How can they help you or mentor you in preparing for the conversation? Reach out to them and ask for the support you need. If all else fails, find a coach to help you prepare and talk through the challenges you may have.

Maybe you are not taking action because you do not see it as painful enough yet for you to do something about it? Here is a practice that may help you. Take a real and honest look at your default future in this company. Your default future is what will happen if you do not make any changes at all.

Write down everything that comes to mind. How painful does it look? Do you actually want this default future? If it is not painful enough, think about it some more and add more notes. Try to get to the point where you look at the list and say: "HELL NO! I will not let this happen to me!"

Although the experience may seem negative, the point here is to give yourself a powerful reason to change. Without a clear reason and purpose to change, it can make it all right to stay where you are now. Knowing what you do not want can help drive you to become more curious about discovering what you DO want in your life.

Earn permission to lead

One of my core beliefs is that leadership is a lot about permission and it is a gift that people give you. You cannot lead anyone unless they give you their implicit permission to do so. So how do you get this gift? Well, there are many different ways:

- How do you treat the people around you?
- Do you words and vision inspire them? Do you share a common dream? Do they want to help you make the dream real?
- Are your intentions, actions, behaviors and words aligned with your vision?
- How consistent are you in showing up this way for the people surrounding you in your life?

The beautiful thing is that because it is a permission people give you, they can also take it away at any time. When they take it away, you are no longer a leader, no matter what you may believe!

The other interesting thing is that being a leader is not the same as being the boss. This is why titles should not matter in defining a leader. Leaders influence people and work in service of something greater than themselves.

In my dormant leader experience, although I had good intentions, people did not always see them. They experienced me as a bully or as someone that always had something to criticize. From my perspective, I was trying to help them deliver better results. From their perspective, I was never satisfied and their work was never good enough. They did not want to give me permission to lead them.

Once I realized the impact that I was having was not aligned to my intentions, it forced me to change. I practiced being more explicit with my intentions and being more spacious with them. Once they realized I was not trying to redo their work but make them look better, things changed.

Step into your personal leadership!

I like to think leadership is something you bring everywhere in your life, not only at work! This is why I think it is useful to refer to this as "personal leadership." It is not about having a title, it is about how you show up everywhere in your life. Work is only one aspect among many others where you can express it.

In his book, *Managing on the Edge*, Richard Pascale defined leadership this way: leadership is making happen what is not going to happen anyway. The statement may feel twisted but it is actually quite powerful.

Bring this back to your own personal leadership in your life. Where are you a dormant leader? Where are you holding back from making things happen? Where are you holding back from jumping in because everyone around you says it will never happen?

Now take a moment and consider—what could happen if you chose to not hold back? What if you started taking charge and have the courage to step into your leadership? What would be different in your life? What impact would you have on the people around you?

Start by getting to know yourself, know your values, know what matters to you! Then go out there and BE the person you want to be and people will decide if they want to follow you. When I say **BE** the person you want to be, I mean do more than just doing actions; instead, live it and breathe it every single day!

Go out there and make the conscious choice to step into your leadership. Choose not to be a dormant leader! Lead in service of something greater than yourself! Face your fears, brush away your excuses, go out there and BE the leader you want to be!

Remember, we only get one life, so we may as well lead a life in which we feel happy and fulfilled!

To close this chapter, let's review some key steps to live a life you want to lead:

- **Step out of your personal prison:** Identify and challenge your limiting beliefs. What would be different in your life if these were not actually true? Work on changing your limiting beliefs to more empowering ones.
- **Choose how you see your life:** Remember that your life will be exactly as you choose to look at it. Change your perspective, change your life! How can you look at your life in a way that opens up more choices and that is more empowering for you?
- **Earn the permission to lead:** No matter how much of a leader YOU THINK you are, you cannot lead anyone unless they give you permission to lead them. How are your behaviors, actions, words, values enabling people to give you permission to lead?
- **Design the life you want:** The life you want will not just magically happen. Think about the life you want to lead. How does it look and feel? Have vision of it that is so rich in your mind that you can feel it and taste it. Then make decisions in your life based on what helps you live your designed life.
- **Step into your personal leadership:** Every day go out and BE the leader you want to be in the world. Remember it is not about being perfect at it, it is about being a more intentional, courageous, and conscious leader every day.

Steffan Surdek

Steffan Surdek is an in-demand leadership development coach and corporate trainer. His drive is to expand the notion of leadership to include each member of the team. As a widely recognized principal consultant, his work has a strong business impact. Steffan helps reshape cultures and guide them in becoming more collaborative and efficient. He is the founder of Pyxis Cultures, a consulting and training company based in Montreal, Canada.

Steffan believes connecting with people at a personal level is the key that allows him to contribute to a greater cause. His passion is to make a real and sustainable difference with his clients in all aspects of their lives.

Steffan often speaks at global conferences about co-creative leadership and the power of teams. His passionate and dynamic storytelling style engages audiences and makes the learning stick. Steffan writes about authentic and co-creative leadership for many different business web sites.

To learn more about Steffan, please visit his website (www.steffansurdek.com) or his leadership blog (www.provokingleadership.com). To learn more about Pyxis Cultures, please visit our web page (www.pyxis-cultures.com)

Twitter: https://www.twitter.com/ssurdek
LinkedIn: https://www.linkedin.com/in/steffansurdek/
Facebook: https://www.facebook.com/steffan.surdek.professional
Web Site: https://www.steffansurdek.com
Leadership Blog: https://www.provokingleadership.com
Pyxis Cultures: https://www.pyxis-cultures.com

BECOME A PERSON OF INFLUENCE
BY NAOMI BAREKET

From a person of numbness to an influencer leader

As a business woman, handling accounts with big companies around the globe, I should have felt excited and successful. Yet something was missing, my soul was numb. I didn't feel that I fulfilled my higher purpose and my real essence of love to give, connect, and inspire. What is success worth when you feel emptiness inside? When at the end of the day you go back home feeling empty with no real impact on other people lives?

I had to check in with myself, connect to my purpose, reminding myself of my natural gifts by looking back to my childhood to see what brought me joy and was my natural strength.

From the time I was a little girl, I had a tendency to see the good in others and in my surroundings. This kind of positive attitude helped me overcome challenges and made me the cheerful girl that always encouraged everybody around me.

Choosing a good attitude doesn't mean you don't face hurdles and challenges. Look at Joseph (Genesis 37) who despite his struggles of being sold into slavery and was in prison, became the leader of all Egypt. **Leaders have a vision that keeps them going through difficult times.** Growing up, my family didn't have much money, but we found room to give to others and spread joy.

My aunt remembers that when I was two years old, I'd run to bring my older brothers' shoes to the door before we went to a walk. I always looked for opportunities to serve others and modeled kindness.

When I was five years old, while my father and I were taking a walk together, we met our old man neighbor who talked nonsense because he was drunk. My father told the drunk neighbor, "You are drunk. You talk nonsense." Although I was only five year old, I told my father, "It is not nice to talk like that to older people." So my father went back with me to the drunk neighbor and apologized. **Leaders can be younger than their followers.** I guess I was sensitive to the needs of others and was willing to help them.

I remember I was assigned to be in charge of my school classmates while we were helping in a local farm. I remember how happy my classmates were when I was assigned to be their leader, and how they collaborated with me to get the best help done for the farm. They trusted me that I wanted the best for all of us. And those I lead still trust me in this same manner.

This kind of positive and uplifting attitude motivates me in inspiring others to shine their unique light on the world.

I have a strong faith in G-d, and I believe He wants us to live a meaningful life and do our unique mission. So I have an inner strong agenda that keeps me devoted on inspiring G-d's creators.

I have this surge of enlightenment that has filled my life with a deeper purpose, meaning, and divine mission, especially knowing that it's not about me but it's about lifting other people's lives.

Visiting my childhood memories, I felt like I'm going back into my real me and purpose. I discovered I wanted to help others to transform lives, inspiring others to find their true purpose as well as inner happiness. I wanted to help them turn their lives from feeling powerless and living as victims of circumstances into feeling in charge and living a meaningful life. I wanted to help them fulfill their unique purpose and manifest the best version of themselves while serving others. And I'm enthusiastic and devoted to this purpose.

Through my experiences, I got this enlightenment that to feel a true fulfillment, to become a real leader, and to become a successful influencer you must have clarity and congruency of your identity, vision, mission, values and beliefs, habits, skills, and environment.

Since I grasped more of what are my essence, my strengths, passion, and higher purpose, I've initiated women empowerment groups, spoken about leadership and empowerment, given empowerment trainings, and became a success mentor for many. I've co-founded a social business venture in Nigeria to empower impoverished Africans to get ahead in life, giving them an opportunity for a fresh start! I've formulated specialized mindset training to help beneficiaries to break through their limitations, tap into their innate creativity, and become independent and successful entrepreneurs. These are based on NeuroSUCCESSology™ –Mission Driven Lives , a company I co-founded and a unique updated method to reach success and fulfillment. My training seminars sell out to audiences from around the globe and I'm touted by my clients as an influential leader in personal growth and achievement.

Leadership expanded my vision and reached internationally.

At the same time, life is a journey and it took some life experience to run a meaningful and leadership filled life.

In order to lead others you must know how to lead yourself first.

I had to contribute more to society to become a leader, a real influencer.

As a speaker, author, and success mentor, the responsibility that I carry on my shoulders is huge. As an influencer I know that my role in the act is to be a leader, a role model and it's always in the back of my mind. Whatever I think, say, and do, always is supported by the saying you can't give what you don't have. We are all leaders in our life; some can be leaders in their workplace, among their friends or family, but what I learn is that first of all we are leaders to ourselves. When you look at the eyes of the person looking back at you from the mirror, what do you see? What do you feel? I learned that before you can become a positive influencer and leader to be followed, first you need to check in with your values and higher purpose, and to like and trust yourself.

In order to become a strong leader and influencer, I learned that I must control the input into my life. I cut down on the news, and I don't waste time on listening to gossiping.

I learned that just as I encourage others, I need to encourage myself and not be harsh and self-judgmental. Rather I must learn from my mistakes.

As a parent, I noticed that my children do what I do rather than what I say they should do. I also noticed the same with my students, trainees, customers, and followers. When they see me daring to speak on stage or author a book, they are more likely to do it too than if I don't do it and only tell them to do it.

Knowing who I am, and being honest with myself, I noticed that naturally I love to bring people together and bring joy to people. I learned that I don't have fun if I don't give or contribute to others. I feel bored, numbed, and meaningless if I don't push others to fulfill their potential.

Every time I speak or give a training, I learn something new from my audience, even basic things, such as human behavior, different human preferences, how I can deliver better and be more vulnerable, and so much more. I never look down on people, and I know that everyone has his/her unique gifts.

I learned to communicate better and to be aware of my triggers. As a mediator, you have to know that when people speak about what is on their mind, it is not about you and you must listen without being defensive or taking everything personally. This can be truly dangerous, and you might lose people's trust, followers, and clients. **Leadership is about being attentive to their needs.**

Throughout my school and college education, I often learned to be competitive and to compare my grades and performances to others. As I'm growing, I'm learning that I should compete against my own abilities and potential and that life is about collaborating and that you can't achieve things without the help of others.

I learned that being a victim takes me nowhere. **Life happens for me and not to me.** It is my responsibility to learn and grow from the challenges.

I used to have limiting beliefs, such as someone else is so lucky because he/she came from a richer family and had a better start, but I learned to accept what is not under my control and to **do my best** of what it is.

The more I'm **true to my real self** and my divine soul and purpose, the happier I am and the more I shine my light on the world.

In order to be a true influencer you must get out of your comfort zone. When I'm invited to speak somewhere far, I want to remain cozy at my home, but when I remind myself that I'm here on earth to live a meaningful life and give value to others, I say yes, and I travel far to speak.

Become the leader of your own self.

All Changes Start with Leadership of Self First. Before we lead others, we need to lead ourselves. Leaders can be negative or positive. Positive leaders have a moral vision and purpose. They care about giving values to society and others.

I believe that like everything else that is operating in our world, you always need the help of others. Even the bed you are sleeping in was man-ufactured by someone else. **Leadership is not about "I", but about "WE", "TOGETHERNESS." It is not about YOU versus ME but all of US together, collectively, to make a change and follow a higher vision.**

Therefore, you need the help of a great team, you need to have great relationships with people, and have great communication skills to keep everyone devoted to the higher vision. And YOU must **BELIEVE** in them and in you.

A leader is someone who believes in you and leads you to shine out your best gifts and performances, so you can reach a higher purpose, vision, and goals.

There are nine secrets in becoming a great leader. It is just like a mother carrying a child for nine months of pregnancy, before the baby is born and shines his/her unique light.

When you are carrying your baby it is not just about you anymore; you have responsibility for the baby and their surroundings too.

Nine secrets for a great leader:

1. **Watch out for the input you put into you, what you expose yourself to**. In the Bible it says: "Judges and officers shall you make for yourselves in all your gates" (Deuteronomy 16:18).
   Focus on goodness and the team's growth in pursuing moral goals.
   Don't be part of gossiping.
   Watch out for your self-talk too. Encourage yourself, and don't put yourself down.

2. **Have self-discipline, determination, and keep your motivation up. Lead by setting an example and being a model to others.**
   Who you are is who you attract. Rule by example. In Joshua 24, after leading his people into a new land, Joshua offers the Israelites the option to either serve G-d or idols. "But as for me and my house," Joshua says, "we will serve the Lord." All the people follow Joshua to serve God. Because they believe in Joshua's leadership, they follow Joshua's example. He inspires them by his example.
   Be passionate and enthusiastic (Enthusiastic means with G-d. Work with G-d's guide in your heart). Make sure to connect and update your motivational factors. Show passion and motivation in your saying and doing. This will be addictive to your followers too.

3. **Be patient, respect other people's model of the world,** and yet push others to fulfill their potential and lift them up. "Be sure you know the condition of your flocks, give careful attention to your herds" (Proverbs 27:23).

4. **Be humble; don't let pride blind you from others' needs.** Teachers learn from their students too. It is said that Moses, regardless of how big of a leader he was, was the humblest man on earth (Numbers 12:3).

5. **Know how to communicate effectively.**
   Know how to listen. "Seek first to understand, then to be understood." In Proverbs 18:13, we read, "He who answers before listening – that is his folly and his shame." Solomon talks about those who wouldn't really listen: "A fool finds no pleasure in understanding but delights in airing his own opinions" (18:2).
   Be aware of selective listening, know what triggers you, and focus on the talker's feeling rather than yours. A leader must listen and respond with a mind that is open and searching for a fuller meaning.
   "Death and life are in the power of the tongue" (Proverbs 18:21).
   Wise leaders think before they speak (have self-control). "Reckless words pierce like a sword, but the tongue of the wise brings healing" (12:18). "A fool gives full vent to his spirit, but a wise man quietly holds it back" (29:11). "A soft answer turns away wrath, but a harsh word

stirs up anger. The tongue of the wise uses knowledge rightly, but the mouth of fools pours forth foolishness" (15: 1-2).

Look for common ground. Focus on the other person, try to understand his or her viewpoint before sharing your own. Ask questions to clarify things you aren't sure of.

6. **Be a good influencer.**

   Know your priorities. Together we can change the world. Great leaders must possess courage and not be afraid of what others think. Deborah was the courageous female Judge who accompanied Barak in the battle showed that she trusted G-d and had no fear of others but only feared G-d (Judges 5:8).

   Be clear about the vision. And follow it. Have strategy and faith; look how David defeated Goliath (1 Samuel 17). David had faith, and despite the giant size of Goliath, David found a way to reach his goal. David put a rock in his sling and swung one of the rocks at Goliath's head. It is a lesson of courage, faith, and overcoming what seems impossible.

7. **Leaders must constantly improve themselves and their skills.**
   a. Learn from the past.
   b. Be open to feedback.
   c. Take responsibility, be in charge. So much easier to blame and come with excuses, rather be in charge and improve.

   Just like the saying do everything as if it all depends on you, and pray to G-d as if everything depends on Him. If you want to increase your influence, you'll invest in your abilities. The more skilled a leader is, the more they'll find themselves in demand. Leaders grow.

8. **Know your values and be kind: "...the Lord looks on the heart"** (1 Samuel 16:7). Have integrity and faith. "Above all else, guard your heart, for everything you do flows from it" (Proverbs 4:23).

9. **See the opportunities for growth in any obstacle you face.** G-d told Abraham in Genesis 12: "Go forth from your country, and from your relatives and from your father's house, to the land which I will show you." In other words, Abraham left his comfort zone and moved on into uncertainty. Great leaders step out of their comfort zone and overcome obstacles.

We are G-d's vessel, so be sure to be an ethical and powerful leader aligned with your gifts and purpose.

"Before I formed you in the womb I knew you, before you were born I set you apart; I appointed you as a prophet to the nations" (Jeremiah 1:5).

Step into your purpose and influence!

Naomi Bareket

NAOMI BAREKET, MBA, is a speaker and dynamic seminar leader who uses modern techniques and Kabalistic studies to facilitate women to own their power and take charge of their minds to create emotional freedom. Bareket is the co-creator of NeuroSUCCESSology™ whereby she offers her broad experience in linguistics, Time Line Therapy®, hypnosis, neuro-science, and the field of Neuro Linguistic Programming (NLP) to empower women to create lives of fulfillment. She has been certified by John Maxwell as a Leadership Coach, Teacher, Trainer, and Speaker, and she is certified by the American Board of NLP to train and certify others as NLP practitioners and as Masters level NLP practitioners.

Bareket is also the author of THE DEEP SEE: *How to See into your Soul and Find Who You Are and Want to Be.* She loves to combine business with spiritual work. Therefore, she loves to work with entrepreneurs. Naomi believes that when you live in alignment with your true self, you can fulfill your life's purpose and live a meaningful life.

naomi@naomibareket.com
443-248-0014
www.naomibareket.com
Facebook: https://www.facebook.com/successology.Neuro
LinkedIn: https://www.linkedin.com/in/naomi-bareket-92b57321
Twitter: @nsuccessgy (https://twitter.com/nsuccessgy)
YouTube: https://www.youtube.com/channel/UCO3UZ5ekNbfoNpt OIrW0G3Q
Instagram: @neurosuccessology

BE WILLING TO BE SEEN, HEARD, AND SHINE!
BY REBECCA HALL GRUYTER

I believe you are called to be Seen, Heard, and SHINE! Especially as leaders, it is important that your people can see you, hear you, and see that it is safe to have an impact. I have discovered that if they cannot see you and they cannot hear you, then they cannot follow you. As long as we stay in hiding behind, behind the scenes—not willing to step out in front—then our impact will be limited. I celebrate you leaning into your leadership style, gifts, and abilities—now be willing to step forward, be seen, and SHINE (share out your vision, gifts, talents, and abilities).

What does it mean to "Step Forward?"

For me, step forward means **to step into what it is you are being called to do**. It means saying "yes" to being seen and to serve. There are fears and there will be challenges, yet you are pulled by your vision to go forward, to touch the lives of others, to share and care in wondrous ways.

Former First Lady Michelle Obama comes to mind, as she shared in her book, *Becoming*. When Barack was making the decision to run for President, Michelle felt very uncertain about this step. She had a family, a career, a life she enjoyed with her husband, and she knew all of that would change the moment he announced his candidacy. However, after deep reflection she realized that this was what they were called to do. So, she stepped forward and leaned in, knowing her "why" but not knowing where this journey would take her and her family.

Leading means **to show up, perfect in our "imperfections."** If all of the famous leaders and influencers waited until everything was in place, every single mistake they could make was made, their future plans had all of the t's crossed and i's dotted, I believe they never would have made any change happen at all! Besides, what seem like "imperfections" to us might just be our strengths to others. I discovered it's about true and real connection, not perfection.

For a long time I hid one of my gifts because it felt like it was an "imperfection". I chose to hide my laugh because I was told it wasn't professional and I became very self-conscious of it. Until one day, a coach told me that it was part of who I am and to embrace it. He shared that when you have something that is contagious, makes people smile, they remember and associate with you then that is not only a gift but a huge asset to you to connect powerfully. He shared, that in fact, laugh more. For the first time, I felt empowered to embrace my laugh. People leaned in to me, I lifted their spirits, they smiled and laughed with me—connecting in heart, life and spirit. How many times do we hide what we see as an imperfection or liability, when in fact that unique thing is the very thing people associate with us and lean into?

Leaning in means **to be willing to be seen and heard**, to be visible. Sometimes the journey to being visible can be uncomfortable and make you feel vulnerable. But think about this: What if by doing that uncomfortable, difficult, scary thing, you made a difference for another person? Or maybe hundreds or thousands of people? That is your potential power of showing up and sharing your gifts. Be willing to SHINE means sharing your gifts, talents, and abilities in such a way that people know what you stand for and you are easy to find.

We again learn an important lesson from Michelle Obama, because while she stepped up to being what turned out to be VERY visible, she did it on her own terms. She alone created what being First Lady would look like, who she would show up to be, authentically and in integrity. She made her role her very own in how she raised her daughters, the change-making projects she chose to work on, the garden she developed on the White House lawn, how she could be an empowering voice for women and girls everywhere, and in many other ways.

Yes, she was often pushed outside of her comfort zone and sometimes faced ugly criticism and judgment. Yet she leaned in, and many of her good works are still going strong today and she is one of the most important and beloved influencers in the world.

We get to make that choice too—how we are going to show up in just the way we are gifted to serve, as the unique and beautifully made individuals that we are! When we lean in and choose, whatever happens to us can become the fuel that propels us toward our purpose.

Being Visible

I want to share with you some things about being visible that leaders and influencers don't often talk about.

When we choose to show up and lean in to leadership, we take on the responsibilities and aspects of visibility. While there are the most beautiful and unexpected gifts that visibility brings us, I want to talk about the aspects we likely do not invite, and certainly did not expect!

At first, I was hesitant to lead. It's a big responsibility and I wasn't sure I wanted to be visible. Well, let's face it, I didn't want to be seen at all! But my urge to serve was stronger than my fear of being seen. And the more I leaned in, the more I learned, and the more I stepped into my role of expert and influencer on a global level.

When you lean into visibility, you learn quickly that you can't possibly control who sees you, how they hear you, or how they're going to react to you or your business. When I began hosting my Women's Empowerment Conferences, I received A LOT of advice and feedback. So much of it was something I welcomed and which helped me grow. However, the more I was visible, the more it began to feel overwhelming to be available to so many people, most of whom wanted the best for me and some who definitely did not. I wanted to serve and to receive and to grow in my service, yet I started to feel my energy draining from me and like I was losing myself within the flurry of ideas and attention: Who do I listen to? Am I not making good decisions myself? Is what they're saying right for me...or not?

I had to stop, pause, reflect, and discover how I would handle this unexpected aspect of visibility.

Find ways to allow people in and serve, while preserving your boundaries.

I discovered that it's not my job to please everybody; sounds simple, doesn't it? As vulnerable as that might make you feel, know that you cannot step onto center stage as an expert or influencer without taking a stand, and that stand simply won't please everybody!

It is important to know and keep your boundaries, and go forward with the awareness that people will say and feel a lot of things about you and your business. **Don't get caught up in what others say.** Stay aware and observe where there's truth and where there isn't. Take in what will serve your brand, business, and life, and kindly release what will not. One phrase I've found that helps me keep my boundaries is: "I can really see how you feel this way; however, this is what we do here." Or "Thank you for sharing." Or "I'll take that into consideration."

Know that you will get known, so be ready!

I have observed that being a leader and gaining visibility changes things in my life. People I don't know come up to me in stores or restaurants, or contact me on the internet or call me on the phone; my inbox is always full. I love how their lives seem to be touched by my work, how wonderful they are, and how fulfilling my work and life are because of the amazing people I serve. At the same time, I sometimes find that I can't go some places and just be, which can be sad and a little bit frustrating. But this is a small cost, for the opportunity, honor, and responsibility we can have as visible leaders to have great impact.

Part of this is because people may see you as your "brand," not as yourself. That you are seen and heard by more than just you—it's what you represent, everything you do and say, and it's weighted and judged according to that perspective. It is important to be aware of this as you step onto a bigger stage. With this awareness, I have crafted boundaries around my public persona and my private one, which has been very helpful in keeping me grounded and focused on the things that matter most to me.

You may find, like I have, that carving out times and places of privacy is a very important practice. One day, my car was in the repair shop and I found that I had some—rare—free time waiting for it to be ready. I wandered around a mall (when was the last time I was in a mall??), just strolling, window-shopping and people-watching. It felt weird and funny and freeing to wander around anonymously with nothing to do and no agenda!

That evening I took some time to pause and notice what that experience had felt like, and as a result I committed to creating more pockets of free time for myself and my husband. Time to just be and not have to do. Keep this practice in mind if you ever find yourself losing your identity to your business image and craving more privacy in your life, feeling crushed or claustrophobic by so much attention.

Find ways to support your "new normal."

As much as you may love the work you're doing, and the people you are serving and collaborating with, it is also very important to make time for yourself personally—again, to be aware of boundaries between your professional and personal life. Bring fresh and different experiences to yourself, and find those opportunities to just BE, to feel freedom and movement and quiet support. Michelle Obama talks about this in her book too, how she made it a point to create regular social time with her best and oldest friends, sometimes just pizza and conversation at the White House residence.

Many of us set aside our hobbies, leisure activities, travel, book clubs, and social dates when we're steeped in growing our business or building a cause. We sometimes are working hard at being a good leader and operate differently from who we are.

To be a great leader is to own who you are and to be the very best you. The world needs all of you, including the you that is healthy, active, creative, and playful! Own your leadership, step forward, and do it the best and most wonderful way in which you are made!

Learn to Dance with Fear

I mentioned earlier that leaning in to leadership and visibility can cause you to feel vulnerable and bring up fears you never knew you had.

I'm sometimes asked, "How do you overcome fear?" I believe we frequently feel fear when we are stretched out of our comfort zone. So, it isn't necessarily something we need to overcome, but we need to discover how to move through it. The first step is to recognize that *fear is a feeling and an indicator that we are stepping outside our comfort zone*—not an indicator that we are in mortal danger (remember, the brain doesn't know the difference between real or imagined danger). With this awareness, we can even see fear as a good sign that we are growing and moving into new spaces.

Have you ever noticed that the more you try to avoid fear, the more it seems to grow and take you over? As I've grown in my business, leadership and visibility, I have learned that it just doesn't work to avoid or run from fear, so instead I choose to "dance" with fear—move with it and through it.

Dancing with fear is critical if we want to move through our comfort zone to bigger visibility and influence. If we want to reach people we haven't reached yet, then we need to be willing to lean in, show up, and share in spaces we haven't shared before. Trust me, dancing with fear in this way will help you serve powerfully.

This is another choice you get to make: If you want to go where you haven't been before and serve in new ways, then you're choosing to move out of your comfort zone. It is your choice to move out or stay where you are. If you choose the status quo, you will have to expect that you will not be moving forward or more into who you fully are as a leader, expert, influencer, or human being.

Be willing to be a little fearful and uncomfortable (for a while) to build what you're called to build and be what you're called to be. Just take one (dance) step at a time, pulled forward by your purpose of bringing truth, empowerment, choice, and value into someone's life. Fear is temporary—the rewards of the dance last a lifetime! Be willing to be seen, heard, and SHINE!

Leadership Tips:

1. **Be willing** to step forward and lean in.
2. **Be willing** to be seen and heard (visible).
3. **Be willing** to share your gifts.
4. **Be willing** to become move visible, truly and authentically be seen.
5. **Be willing** to create balance and boundaries in your life.
6. **Be willing** to go where you haven't gone before and dance with fear.
7. **Be willing** to SHINE!

Rebecca Hall Gruyter

Rebecca Hall Gruyter (CEO of Your Purpose Driven Practice and RHG Media Productions) specializes in highlighting experts to help them reach more people around the world! From the Speaker Talent Search (that helps you find more speaking opportunities), podcast opportunities (syndicated on multiple networks), to writing opportunities including bringing your book forward as a best seller.

She is an award-winning #1 international best-selling author multiple times over, published in over five magazines and over 20 books to date plus two more to be released in 2019. A popular talk radio show host/producer, dynamic TV show host/producer, creator of the Women's Empowerment Conference Series and an in-demand guest expert and speaker.

Rebecca has been recognized by CBS, ABC, Fox, and NBC as a top professional in the area of Purpose Driven Entrepreneurship. With a promotional reach of over 10 million, she is committed to helping you reach more people around the world as you step into a place of Influence! Remember, what the world needs is more of YOU!

(925) 787-1572
Rebecca@YourPurposeDrivenPractice.com
www.facebook.com/rhallgruyter (Facebook)
www.linkedin.com/pub/rebecca-hall-gruyter/9/266/280 (LinkedIn)
www.YourPurposeDrivenPractice.com (Main Website)
#RHGTVNetwork (Instagram)
www.RHGTVNetwork.com (TV Network)
www.twitter.com/Rebecchgruyter (Twitter)
www.SpeakerTalentSearch.com (Free Opportunity for Speakers to get on More Stages)
www.EmpoweringWomenTransformingLives.com (Weekly Radio Show)
www.MeetWithRebecca.com (Calendar link to schedule a time to talk with Rebecca)

SECTION 2:

Your Leadership Toolbox

THE NEUROSCIENCE OF LEADERSHIP:
THE POWER OF WORDS AND ACTIONS
BY JULIE ANDERSON

What makes a great leader? Is it charisma? Or maybe commanding a strong presence? Perhaps it is confidence or poise. **In reality, a truly great leader has qualities that draw people to them.**

Qualities that shine in such a way that people want to listen to what they say and are motivated to act on it. Many individuals are in a leadership position even if they don't have a title of "leader."

You may be looked up to as a leader in your community, family, or school. Or perhaps you are in a formal position as a leader in your career or business. Whether you have that formal title or not, there is a huge responsibility and honor to be in a position of leadership.

For many years now I have been sharing with individuals, groups, and corporations the amazing information that is coming out of the field of neuroscience connected to how the functioning of our brains help us to understand who we are and why we do the things that we do. In doing this, I have fallen into a leadership position. A position that I love and do not take lightly. **Knowing that the information I share and the manner in which I share it can change people's lives is a big responsibility. One**

that I value and hope never to take for granted. At times I do have to put myself in check. I can get so excited about the information that I neglect the application of the information. For me I have to go back over the points that I am sharing with you in this chapter. My hope is that this information will be as valuable to you as I have found it for me. With that in mind, let me share with you just a few of my favorite findings.

Applied neuroscience (the science of how our brains are each uniquely designed and wired) is revealing so much to us about our brain and human behavior. When we learn how to tap into the natural brain gifts that we as individuals have and then work at inspiring others to shine in their natural gifts every endeavor in our life becomes more rewarding. This is especially true when it comes to your position as a leader. If you are choosing to step into a leadership role in your life or business, you are to be commended.

Leadership is so much more than just leading a group of people. Leaders have influence over those that look to them. **This power of influence should never be taken lightly. Things that you say and do can affect people deeply for the positive and if you are not careful, for the negative.** Neuroscience is helping us to see just how powerful what we say is. Depending on the level of influence you have in a person's life you can affect their brain chemistry. In fact, if you have a strong influence in their life you can even affect their brain wiring. When you keep this in mind you can lift and empower people to brave new heights. Inspiring them with actions, words, and thoughts that will help influence their brain in a positive and powerful way.

The Power of Words

Let's look at some of the science surrounding how our brain reacts to just words that we meditate on. In their book *The Power of Words*, Dr. Andrew Newberg, a neuroscientist at Thomas

Jefferson University, and Mark Robert Waldman, a communications expert. "*a single word has the power to influence the expression of genes that regulate physical and emotional stress.*" They discovered that when we use positive words like "love," "peace," and "loving-kindness," we can increase cognitive reasoning and strengthen areas in our frontal lobes. **Using positive words more often than negative words can activate the**

motivational centers of the brain. Simply put, it can alter the chemistry in our brains in positive ways.

Researchers at Harvard University discovered that positive words related to rewards, victory, or security can trigger the production of oxytocin. Oxytocin is the neurochemical that bonds people and gives feelings of well-being and safety. In fact, neuroscientists have noted that meditating on positive words and sayings can alter your basic brain functions as well. Functions in the parietal area (the portion of the brain that processes sensory information, interprets visual information, and processes language and math) of the brain change. This changes your perception of yourself and the people that you interact with. In general, you develop a more positive view of yourself and others. You, in fact, develop a bias toward seeing the good in people.

It is just as important to pay attention to what happens when negative words are focused on.

When negative words become the focus, you can prevent your brain from producing certain neurochemicals that contribute to stress management. It also increases the activity in your brain's fear center, the amygdala. The amygdala next hijacks your brain, shuts down the logical thinking portions of the brain, and causes stress-producing hormones to flood your system. This in turn alters your self-perception in a negative way. It leads to a more negative self-image and you tend to become more suspicious of others.

Fascinating information and powerful when you apply it to your position of leadership. I tell people that I work with that there is no greater damage done to an individual's self-esteem or feelings of self-worth than the insignificant things said to them by significant people in their lives. **When you are in a leadership position, you are in a significant position in the lives of the people who are following you. To know that the very words that you use when interacting with them can have the power to alter their brains and their relationships in such a way can be sobering.** Yet when applied in the right way, the power of your words can have a tremendously positive impact on their lives. In turn that release of oxytocin in their brains will bond them to you in a positive way.

This is a good time for some self-reflection. Take a few moments, grab a pen and paper, and jot down some thoughts. Ask yourself: What words can I say that will encourage others to achieve their greatness? How can

I shape my message with such positivity that it will improve the lives of those who listen? Do I take seriously the power of the words I use to shape others' lives?

When we pay attention and improve in this area, we can transition from being an okay leader to becoming a GREAT leader.

The Power of Your Actions.

When it comes to leadership, your actions are just as important as the words that you use.

Actions, like words, can alter the brain in positive or negative ways. Once again, I turn to neuroscience to help you get the picture and feeling of the importance of your interaction with others. I refer to the part of the brain I mentioned earlier, the amygdala. It is an important part of the brain to consider when discussing the topic of your actions and your body language as you interact with others. When the amygdala takes over it can result in negative responses in the brain and body. Something that you need to keep in mind in your leadership position.

The amygdala is responsible for protecting us. It activates whenever it feels that the body it oversees is threatened. Now it is important to note that the amygdala does not know the difference between real stress and perceived stress. This means that while you may not present a

REAL threat to those who follow you, if there is a perceived threat based on your actions their amygdala will respond accordingly. If your body language is overbearing or you give those around you a feeling of superiority, it could set the "fear" sensor in their brain off. Then the amygdala takes over.

Try not to let this discourage you in any way. **It just means that you need to be aware of the influence you have and how your actions will affect other people.** Beware of giving off the feeling to others that they are bothering you. Keep open body language and good eye contact.

Acknowledge others' feelings even when you feel that they are unfounded. Remember that a person's perspective is based on their brain wiring. Something seemingly small and unimportant to you may be HUGE to the person you are interacting with. Next time you are in a conversation with someone, pay attention to how you are acting. What is your body language telling them? Are you keeping good eye contact with the person indicating interest? How are they responding to you? Are they leaning in with open, accepting body language or are they closed and withdrawn?

Paying attention to these cues will help you to increase your effectiveness as a great leader.

It is also important that you become as approachable as you can be. Take public speaking, for example. You can do a great job on the platform using great positive words to inspire people then undo all that good as soon as you walk off the stage. I often attend conferences and enjoy hearing the wisdom that experts share. What really impresses me the most is when you have a presenter who stays after their presentation and really connects with their audience.

However, it is annoying to me when I see someone who quickly exits or ignores people who have a genuine interest in learning more or simply connecting with them. It can be damaging to a leader's relationship with their followers if they are not approachable. It can send a message to the listeners' brain that they are not worthy of the leader's time. Depending on the current self-worth a person has you can just imagine how devastating this might be. **When you work at being open and approachable the positive effect you have on the lives of those around you can be huge.**

Think Receiver, Not Sender

One last point that will have a powerful impact on your effectiveness as a leader is this point:

Think receiver, not sender. What exactly do I mean by this? As a Brain Personality Connection

Expert one of the key things that I teach is the importance of becoming intimately connected to your natural brain gifts. In learning this you also find that your gifts are unique, and your brain, based on its wiring, will process information and rate importance on things the way it is wired.

However, **each person has their own Brain Personality Connection.** While there are similarities or general personality categories, one thing you cannot generalize is a person's life experience. How I perceive things may be completely different than how you perceive things just based on the different life experiences we have had.

This is never to say that one way is any better than another, it is just simply different. This is so important to keep in mind as you fulfill your leadership role. **We naturally interact with and respond to what I call our brain default. This default can be completely different from those around you or those you are speaking with.** Take a few moments to think about your approach. When preparing information to share with others do you focus on their needs? Do you look and meditate on how you can empower and inspire them in ways that their brain will receive it? How do you need to approach situations in a way that will make people feel comfortable, understood, and inspired? When you keep these points in mind your effectiveness as a leader will take a large leap forward.

In conclusion, I hope that this information will help you to increase your effectiveness and impact you as a leader. The gift to transform lives for the better is an amazing one. The individuals you will touch with your message and the people you will inspire will forever be changed by your presence in their lives. Engage your brain. Train it to work for the people you serve. The end result will be powerful when you do.

Neuroscience Leadership Tips:

1. As a leader, you have influence and impact on those around you.
2. Be aware of and mindful of the power of your words and actions.
3. Remember to think "Receiver" not "Sender."
4. You have the gift to transform lives.
5. Share your gifts fully and powerfully as you lead and SHINE!

Julie Anderson

Julie Anderson is also known as the "Brain Lady" Speaker.

Julie Anderson is an in-demand international public speaker; wielding her expertise in brain science to bring solution-based training into organizations and with entrepreneurs for business, communications, relationships, and life success resulting in increasing productivity, skyrocketing sales, preventing conflicts, and breaking through barriers in business and life.

An established brain authority in the media, Julie has been interviewed by ABC, FOX, UPN, and is a frequent expert guest on many radio networks. She is also host of the Brain Lady Speaks radio show on the EWN Podcast network. Julie has done extensive research in the areas of personality types, brain function and anatomy, brain health, and the brain personality connection.

She has studied natural health, psychology, human resource development, and psychoneuroimmunology. She has more than 20 years of research, study, mentoring, and sharing the stage with other gurus in the field of brain personality connection. She has continuing education credits in the field of depression, anxiety disorders, and brain function. Julie has continued her learning to maintain her expertise in the field of neuroscience and neuropsychology. She is also a professional interpreter for the deaf.

Julie Anderson brings more than 20 years of experience speaking, training, and consulting with individuals, entrepreneurs, women's groups, and large corporate organizations utilizing Brain Personality Connection and uniquely blending science and psychology with humor and relatability in her keynote presentations and interactive workshops.

For a complete list of organizations Julie has presented for as well as comments and testimonials from clients, please go to www.BrainLadySpeaker.com or email Julie at Info@BrainLadySpeaker.com or call 530-913-4407.

Email Address: info@BrainLadySpeaker.com
Phone Number: 530-913-4407
Website/products and services: www.YourBestMindOnline.com
Website for booking Brain Lady to speak:
www.BrainLadySpeaker.com
Facebook: https://www.facebook.com/purplebrainlady/
and https://www.facebook.com/YourBestMindOnline/
LinkedIn: https://www.linkedin.com/in/brainladyjulie/
Twitter: https://twitter.com/BrainLady
You Tube: www.youtube.com/yourbestmind

THE 7 COLORS OF AUTHENTIC LEADERSHIP
BY MONEEKA SAWYER

Brrrrr...the cold air in the wee hours of Monday morning sent shivers up my spine. I rolled to my side and snuggled deep into my pillow. Fifteen minutes later, my alarm clock rang. Bzz! Bzz! Bzz! Holy Cow! That's loud! Drowsily, I flung my arm out and whacked the snooze button. A few minutes later, the alarm clock rang again. I opened one eye and peered into the morning light. It took a minute or two for me to turn the alarm off and get out of bed, but get out of bed I did...and straight into a hot shower.

All dressed up and ready to go, I hustled down the stairs and brewed up some coffee, my first of the day. Ahh...so good! I curled my toes and rocked forward onto the balls of my feet. As soon as my heels touched the floor again, I was moving. With a granola bar clamped between my teeth, I slid into my jacket, swung my purse over my shoulders, grabbed my keys, and bounded through the front door. Look out, world, here I come! Twenty minutes later, I was standing at the head of a long, narrow table in a board-room, surrounded by middle-aged men in power suits! I took a conscious breath, silently thanked the stars for my morning coffee, and began...

Do you think you are not a leader type?
Do you want to be a leader?
When you take on a leadership role, do you feel like a fraud?

Have you ever found yourself confronted with addressing the most pressing issues of a day in front of an adversarial group of people? This is what leaders are often called to do! And yet, they are still composed enough to do this with grace and influence. But how? What is it about leaders that give them the confidence and power to address a boardroom as easily as you might address a birthday party?

If you really want to know then keep reading. Within the next few pages, I will tell you how you can connect with your own innate power and use it to create the ideal environment to accomplish your dreams. So hold on tight and let's get started!

When I was a little girl, I used to stand on the sidelines during recess and look out onto the vast playground where children of all sizes and shapes were engaged in play. I would pay particular attention to the children who seemed to be the leaders in their play groups. They seemed confident and popular and most importantly, happy. Standing under the darkness of the awnings alongside the school building, I decided that I would be one of them someday. But how would I overcome my shyness and cross the cultural barrier that always seemed to stand between them and me?

It wasn't until high school that I came to a turning point. I was going to a school dance and I really wanted to fit in. So I put a lot of effort in dressing up and then drove off into adventure. When I got there, I entered the gym with flare. I had fantasized that I would be the prettiest, most desirable girl in the room and that all the boys I liked would forget their dates and make a beeline straight for me! But my fantasy remained just that – a fantasy. In reality, I ended up standing on the sidelines and looking on as others chatted and took to the dance floor. That night, I decided that I would stop looking to others for confirmation.

From then on, the disappointments didn't hurt as much and my sense of isolation started to fade. I began to delve into the field of psychology to understand why I didn't fit in – and how I could change. I read book after book, experimenting from time to time with some of the strategies that I had learned.

Over the years, I have learned that leaders come in different forms and have many faces. I began to divide them into seven distinct groups and assigned each group a color. The chart below describes what I came up with.

RED	Those who are the pillars of society. They are solid, reliable, and stable.	George Washington Bill Gates
ORANGE	Those who lead with creativity, playfulness, and joy.	Maya Angelou Ellen DeGeneres Princess Diana
YELLOW	Those who are powerful, confident, and inspire awe.	Oprah Jean Luc Picard Margaret Thatcher
GREEN	Those who lead with connection, collaboration, and compassion.	Mother Teresa Nelson Mandela
BLUE	Those who lead with their words.	President John F. Kennedy Dr. Martin Luther King, Jr.
INDIGO/ NAVY BLUE	Those who lead with knowledge.	Chancellor Angela Merkel Thomas Edison
WHITE	Those who lead by showing us how to elevate our Spirit.	Mahatma Gandhi Buddha Joan of Arc

Each of the examples that I have listed have a combination of leadership styles. I have simply aligned them with their dominant style and corresponding color. The same goes for each of us. We all have a way that we prefer to be in the world and this is the way that we are most comfortable being when we are in a leadership role.

You all know that you are all leaders, right? You know that you were born to lead. But did you know that you have a leadership ecosystem in your body? Your mind, your emotions, and your physiology are all part of this ecosystem. And the most important part of this ecosystem is your energy system.

Think of your ecosystem as a house. There are many things that make that house what it is. It's structure. It's aesthetic. How it's decorated. All the conveniences inside. It may have gorgeous flooring, plush carpets, top notch appliances, a gorgeous garden, but what happens when the power goes out? How comfortable is it then? How functional is it? A house without electricity still serves the purpose of a house, but it isn't a blissful home. It isn't functioning at 100%. The same goes for the energy system in your body, what I call the Pillar of Perfection. Everything can be in good working order, but without the necessary energy, it is lifeless.

This energy system is our chakra system. Chakras are powerful energy centers that affect the physical, mental, and emotional well-being of the physical body. There are seven major chakras in the human energy body, and they are arranged vertically along the spine, starting at the base and moving up through the top of the head.

As shown in the chart below, each chakra has a specific name and a corresponding color associated with it. In addition, each chakra has a specific sound signature. For instance, the sacral chakra, the one located just below your belly button, corresponds to the color orange, and the sound vaam.

CHAKRAS: Energy Centers in the body

NAME	COLOR	LOCATION	SOUND
Root	Red	Base of spine	Laam
Sacral	Orange	Lower abdomen, below the navel	Vaam
Solar Plexus	Yellow	Upper abdomen, above the navel	Raam
Heart	Green	Center of the chest	Yaam
Throat	Blue	Base of the throat	Ham
Third Eye	Indigo/ Navy Blue	Lower forehead, between the eyebrows	Au
Crown	White	Just above the top of the head	Mmm

In your energy system, each chakra governs a particular area of your life. If it is blocked, that area will not function at its best. And because the chakras are all part of your Pillar of Perfection, it affects all the others and nothing will work at its best.

Therefore, it's important that we keep all our energy centers open and unblocked. And if all these centers are open, then together they can support us in being the most powerful leader we can be in our preferred color style.

Take a look at the two charts I presented above. What do you notice? There are seven main chakras, and each one of them corresponds to one of the colors of leadership. These seven chakras are the building blocks of your Pillar of Perfection. Once these centers are clear, and your Pillar of Perfection is strong, everything else works more smoothly and you are able to fully stand in your own natural, innate power. We are able to fully step forward as a leader in our own unique way.

Would you like to learn how to strengthen your Pillar of Perfection?

Remember true leadership starts from the inside out.

If you open up your chakras, you will attract everything you want in your life. You will command respect, stand in your power, and be seen as an authentic leader. If you are not able to be your most powerful authentic self, people will subconsciously be able to tell. They may intellectually think of you as a leader, but they may not want to follow you. Or if they do follow, they may not stay long. A true leader must be true to themselves in order to be able to lead long-term. That's why we must focus on what is going on inside of you, at the deepest level first.

Keep in mind that it is very important to clear all the chakras, because if you just clear one, it will get muddled up quickly by the unclear energies of the other chakras. But we have to start somewhere, and for us women the best place to start is in the sacral chakra. This is our feminine power center. It is located a couple inches below your belly button.

This is our place of creation. From this place we give birth. We give birth to children. We give birth to ideas. We give birth to businesses. This is also a place of creativity, playfulness, and joy. This is the chakra that enhances the feminine power of attraction. The feminine attracts and receives, while the masculine pursues and provides.

Would you like to have a little taste of what it's like to clear your sacral chakra? Awesome. To create the Pillar of Perfection we focus on three things: breath, sound, and visualization.

Let's start with breath.

Close your eyes and take in a slow deep breath through your nose. Notice how far down the breath goes. Does it stop in your chest, or maybe even your throat?

Now release it slowly through your mouth.

You're going to take another deep breath in, but this time imagine that breath goes all the way down to tickle the back of your belly button.

Hold that breath for a moment, and then release it slowly through your mouth.

Can you imagine sending mucky energy out to someone? This actually happens all the time. Have you ever been in a really good mood and then chatted with someone and then felt really irritated, distracted, or impatient afterward? That's because you picked up the energy they were radiating out. When you are connecting with people you don't want to be sending out this kind of bad energy, right? You want to make sure when you do this connection exercise, you are balanced and strong and have good energy to share. You are going to connect heart-to-heart with people. Make sure your intentions are loving or the connection can have unexpected negative results.

How to connect energetically with others.

Here is what you do:

1. First, let's clear the heart chakra.
2. Take a couple breaths of bright white air in and out and see the beautiful green rose open up and fill your heart chakra with light.
3. Now as you breathe in imagine that air being infused with your loving powerful heart chakra energy.
4. When you breathe out, imagine sending that breath like a bridge from your heart to the other person's heart.
5. Do this slowly and gently. Bridge the energy of your heart with the energy of theirs. Fill their heart with the loving energy you want to share.

Notice what happens. Often, the other person will visibly relax. They will start to smile. Sometimes even their voice will get a bit higher. It's so much fun to watch them react to our powerful loving energy.

Isn't that amazing? Start practicing this on every single one-on-one interaction you have. See how your communications change. See how people respond to your differently. And watch how this becomes easier and easier.

Leadership at its most basic form is about impacting other people. Through this exercise you are able to impact someone in the most positive loving way possible. And you can expand that impact one person at a time.

Be the authentic leader you were meant to be.

You are a natural leader. Understand what your leadership style is, and allow yourself to lead in that way. Keep it unique to you.

Allow your most powerful loving self to connect with those around you, and you will see how easily and magically you can be the leader you always wanted to be.

* * * *

As I glanced around the table, I noticed the expressions on the faces of these men. They all had scowls on their faces. So, I did what I do best. I smiled my most charming smile, sent my heart energy into the room, and began.

"Well, hello there, everyone! Shall we get started?"

This meeting was set because my partners and I were trying to build a condominium complex and had not been able to get our plans approved from the planning department. The conversation started heatedly, with each man arguing his case.

When it came to me, I said calmly, "You know, we are actually all on the same team. We all want Los Altos to stay beautiful, and we all want something beautiful to go into that empty property so that all the crime currently going on there stops. Handling this will save the city a lot of money in police surveillance as well as meeting everyone's needs."

The men all looked at me dumbstruck. After a pregnant pause, their expressions began to change. I controlled the conversation for the rest of the meeting, and one by one they started nodding their heads. The aspiration of bettering their own community seemed to allay their fears and soften their resolves. I released the breath that I didn't know I had been holding and began to relax. Hope had resurfaced and a solution was in sight!

By the end of our time together, we had a plan in place that we all agreed on and a signed commitment by the planning department controller to approve it.

And VOILA! Sacral Chakra leadership at its best!

Imagine what you could do if you allowed yourself to be the leader you were meant to be.

Moneeka Sawyer

Moneeka Sawyer is often described as one of the most blissful people you will ever meet. She has been investing in real estate for over 20 years, so has been through all the different cycles of the market. Still, she has turned $10,000 into over $2,000,000, working only 5-10 hours per MONTH with very little stress.

While building her multi-million dollar business, she has travelled to over 55 countries, dances every single day, and spends lots of time with her husband of over 20 years and her adorable little puppy (who is the love of her life, but shhhh...don't tell her husband).

Moneeka loves teaching others how to build wealth like she has so they can create the life of their dreams. She's helped parents pay for their children's college educations and weddings. She's helped countless people to retire with the lifestyle they dreamed of. She's helped so many people become millionaires. And they've all done this Moneeka's blissful way.

Moneeka is the best-selling author of the award-winning book *Choose Bliss: The Power and Practice of Joy and Contentment*. She is also the recipient of the Woman of Impact Quill award from Focus on Women Magazine, and the Quill Award for Best Literary Work from the Governor of the State of Maryland.

She is the host of the podcast Real Estate Investing for Women, and her expertise and bliss-filled laugh have been featured on stages, radio, podcasts, and TV stations including ABC, CBS, FOX, and the CW.

To find out more about Moneeka, go to: **Blissfulinvestor.com**

Facebook.com/MoneekaSawyer
Twitter.com/MoneekaSawyer
https://www.facebook.com/groups/blissfulinvestor/
https://www.facebook.com/BlissfulRealEstateInvestor/
https://www.facebook.com/coreblisslifeliveblissfromyourcore/
https://www.facebook.com/groups/alwayschoosebliss/
https://www.linkedin.com/in/moneeka-sawyer-4561145/
https://www.instagram.com/moneekasawyer/

LEADERS, THRIVE THROUGH TRANSITION!
BY PATRICIA RACHEL SCHWARTZ, MA, PCC, BCC

As a leader you experience continuous change and transition. The pace of change has so accelerated that most of us find ourselves in some degree of transition most of the time. If we are in transition then our teams or our organizations are likely reflecting that transition. If change is affecting our organizations then it will affect the individuals in them, including us. Change can originate from various directions creating a domino effect, affecting anything or anyone on its path.

Today, leaders are expected to adapt on an ongoing basis to new realities. The term "VUCA" (volatile, uncertain, complex, ambiguous) which often is used to describe the context in which we are operating, was coined by the military in the 1990s to reflect the accelerated, less stable, and rapidly changing world.

Does VUCA sound like your workday?

My clients are dealing with minor to major new realities like career shifts, mergers, acquisitions and reorganizations/layoffs, job transfers, system changes, a change in company strategy or vision, changes in regulations, the need to retire and pass the torch to the successor, etc. Sometimes several of these changes are going on at the same time. Some people are more comfortable with change than others. Most people experience a sense of threat related to change.

If you would like to be reminded of what you know to be true, or impacted in your thinking about change and transition, this chapter is for you. If you are a small business leader, a leader in a Fortune 500 company, an entrepreneur, a business services professional, consultant, coach, or a nonprofit leader, understanding change and using transition as a path to the future will support your success.

What would it take for you to reduce the sense of threat related to change so you have a greater potential to "shine" through change and transition? Let's start by unpacking change and transition. And then let's explore the range of often time-limited opportunities inherent in successfully navigating transitions.

A change could be abrupt and uninvited. Or it could come about slowly and be chosen. One of my clients, Karen, a VP in a Fortune 500 company, who is also a competitive dancer in her spare time, spends part of every morning before work practicing her dancing. She navigates high levels of daily uninvited change at work. She finds herself and her division in transition on a regular basis and has felt stressed, confused, and irritable. As a result, we discussed and created strategies for her to handle the high levels of change and the transition it creates for her daily. A key to navigating change is having a strategy and tools in place to support you as a leader going through the transition.

Uninvited and/or abrupt change is harder to handle than invited change due to the element of surprise. A change can be positive or negative. Sometimes, change is something you initiate. For example, clients Ana and Joe needed to take their business services company to the next level quickly or it would be in danger of losing its competitive edge. They also had to let a charismatic high-level manager go, leading to a gap in talent at a critical moment. The combined impact of these changes created an even higher level of urgency. We therefore put together a plan to support them and their organization through this transition in a powerful and positive way.

Take a moment to think about the changes that you are experiencing for yourself and in your organization. How are they affecting you?

Transition is what happens to our thoughts and feelings in reaction to change in our environment. Most of us are not completely conscious of this internal process although we know something is going on because of how we feel. My clients report a range of reactions to change such as feeling energized, happy, sad, lighter, angry, afraid, lonely, irritated, relieved, exhausted, incompetent, frustrated, connected, at peace, anxious, lost, confused, out of sorts, serene, etc. Have you ever experienced feelings like these after some kind of change? Probably, because reactions are a normal part of the transition process.

In this chapter I will focus primarily on the significant changes described earlier that create more profound transition experiences. The attention in this brief chapter will be on you as the leader and not so much on those you lead. You can, however, apply the information here when interacting with those at work as well as at home.

Transition is a process that has been studied and written about over time. It has observable phases associated with it. Various transition models exist. Frederic Hudson[1] and William Bridges are thought leaders who have each created useful transition models. Models such as these address the change from the viewpoint of those affected by it. My model is influenced by William Bridges' model[2]. Transition models are different than and work well with Change Management models, like John Kotter's eight stage process[3]. Change Management models help you lead change initiatives in operational areas like preparation, communication, vision sharing, but this chapter is related to transition, the internal experience people have when reacting to a change.

Transition models all refer to stages or phases of transition that we experience universally. The way I identify these phases are: *Release (I was)*, *Reassess and Regenerate (I am)*, and *Results (I will be)* stages. My clients and I have had several insights that I will share with you about how to move through transition in a way where you can thrive.

Here is a summary of the phases of transition as I see them and some ideas for how to handle each phase.

---

[1] Hudson, Frederic M., PH.D, The Handbook of Coaching, Jossey-Bass, San Francisco, 1999

[2] Bridges, William, Transitions, Da Capo Press, Cambridge, MA 2004

[3] Kotter, John P., Leading Change, Harvard Business School Press, 1996

Phase 1: Release (I was)

This is the phase where it is necessary to release or say goodbye to a situation, a relationship, a role, a system, an identity. It is a time of loss. It could be a desired or positive loss. It is still a loss. When you experience a release of a prior role or situation, you might feel sadness or grief, disorientation, anger or resentment, and you might be worried about the future. This is normal when you release the past. This phase is about feeling and completing things.

In this phase, handle anything that is in your power to complete in relation to the people or situations involved, including with yourself, in order to experience closure. Allowing emotions to surface and feeling them is a healthy part of the process. The more profound the change, the more powerful the emotions will be. It is helpful to have support during this phase as in all the phases of transition. An ally, such as a trusted (outside) colleague, friend, or an executive coach can be a great support and thinking partner for you.

As a leader, you will be going through your experience of a release while being called on to support others. Taking time to care for yourself, especially your emotional and physical health, will help you support others.

Phase 2: Reassess/Regenerate (I am)

After the release phase, Reassess/Regenerate is the next phase that I've observed. It is like a bridge or threshold between "I was" and "I will be." The past is over, the change has happened, and the future hasn't begun yet. This is likely familiar as you've probably navigated many situations over the years. This time period works like a seed that is sprouting deep in the earth, but we can't see it until it breaks the surface.

Many connections and structures will have been released in the prior phase. All the behaviors, relationships, and routines associated with the past roles, situations, or relationships change or dissolve. Like Paul, a VP who opted for the golden parachute when the company moved its headquarters out of state and now it is his first (jolting) Monday morning without a job. Or Suzanne, who began her senior leader role at a company the same week they merged with another company. She was already in transition and within days so was everyone else. This phase brings a sense of abundant open space and the attendant issues where daily structures used to be.

If this sounds challenging, it can be! This phase can be an uncomfortable and anxiety-producing place on one hand and also, an extremely rich, fulfilling, nourishing, creative, liberating, satisfying, and transformational space that has the potential for a new vision of possibilities to emerge for the future.

Given that it's a space of the unknown, many of us would like to avoid experiencing the Reassess and Regenerate phase at all costs. This phase is about "being" in the present, which is why I call it the "I am" phase. It is a time to explore and discover what feeds you, your purpose, strengths, values, best experiences, wishes. In this phase you reassess and regenerate you at your best.

If you take some deep reflection time to get to the core of your purpose, to reconnect with your values and your strengths, and to realize how amazing you are as a human being, honoring yourself for this simple fact, this will renew you. If you remind yourself of who you are at your best, especially recalling any past transition experiences where you learned, grew, and perhaps experienced a transformation, you can access your best contributions and bring those parts of yourself more to the forefront as you move ahead.

In this phase I ask leaders like Ralph to take a 10,000 ft. view to see what perspective they can get internally and externally on their organization and marketplace. Ralph imagined himself watching the video from a drone 10,000 ft. above circling his business. He became aware of some strengths and opportunities for innovation. You can leverage this special seedling time too to allow space for a transformation in thinking and perspective leading to innovation.

Innovation and creativity would not have the same urgency in "normal time." In normal time, we do what is urgent, so the long-term vision, values, strengths, creativity, and planning don't always happen. The Reassess/ Regenerate phase presents an opportunity to "be" rather than "do": to reflect deeply, to take thoughts to the end, to slow down, and encourage an environment for insight and transformation to take hold. Creativity and innovation become the urgent imperatives. Because priorities flip, there is power and inspiration available in the darkest hours of transition to access for transformation to the next level for ourselves, our people, and all our stakeholders.

Earlier I mentioned Karen who was struggling with reactions to daily change. She found that when she gets into a rough moment where she might react at work, by using self-awareness she could consciously focus her attention on the dance steps she's learning and it calms her down. Then she can think and decide how to handle the current reality. She surprised everyone in her organization with her newfound poise.

I also introduced you to business partners Ana and Joe who were dealing with up-leveling and the loss of a key staff member. They had a realization that they needed to lead the way to a climate of innovation and embrace the qualities of freedom and creativity available in the Reassess/Regenerate phase. They focused on taming their own demons so they could show up in a confident manner for their remaining team. They reported that they not only reached their goal but also unexpectedly created new roles for themselves in their organization.

In both cases my clients realized the Reassess/Regenerate phase is a time for exploring the internal landscape of their values, strengths, and strategies. Through the thinking partnership of coaching, we came up with ways to leverage their creative power for exploration and renewal leading to unpredictable positive shifts in perspective.

Phase 3: Results (I will be)

As you move through the Reassess/Regenerate phase, you will find yourself naturally in the Results stage. This is where you "do" things again: re-launch yourself or your company perhaps with a refreshed focus or brand; learn new things; maybe search for a new position if applicable; enjoy a sense of openness and curiosity; market your new product. You will have more energy and enthusiasm which will lead you to set and achieve goals. Depending on how much exploration you have allowed yourself in the prior phases, you will be more of you at your best in the Results phase. Paul with the golden parachute realized in the Reassess/Regenerate phase that he wanted to keep working. In this Results phase he prepared the launch of his consulting practice for C-suite leaders in his industry.

By taking actions to help yourself be fully in these stages, you give yourself the possibly to maximize the available creative power. You can harness the anxiety and leverage it into structures that support you by being more aware of how you are feeling and what you are thinking. The opportunity you leverage for deep reflection allows you to exit the transition period with a transformation toward what is most important to you and your work.

Keys to Thriving Through Transition

1. **Choose a "Growth Mindset" (vs. a "Fixed Mindset")**
   Researcher and professor Carol Dweck coined the term "mindset" as well as "fixed" and "growth" mindset[4]. Our mindset is our perspective of our abilities. A growth mindset is the perspective that we can improve our talents and abilities versus a fixed mindset which says our abilities are unchanging. To create the most open, innovative climate for you and those around you, try on a growth mindset, if you do not already subscribe to it. See where it leads you.
2. **Get to know your strengths and talents**
   With a growth mindset you will be able to more fully appreciate the power of your strengths. Learn about your strengths through feedback and taking online assessments. An executive coach can help you dive deeply into learning about you at your best and how to maximize your strengths.
3. **Set a self-awareness and self-management goal**
   You might set a goal to become more aware of your positive or negative thoughts during the day, and turn around negative thoughts. How do you feel? What are you thinking? You need to be aware of how you feel before you can manage your feelings. Try to pause a few times during the day and ask yourself these questions. A leader's emotions and behavior are felt and noticed at all levels of the organization. A top leader's demeanor and mood have about a 70% impact on the climate of a company. Leaders will therefore want to cultivate internal stability in order to effectively handle external change and transition.

I invite you to consider that change and transition offer a unique and powerful opportunity to take stock of your past and present to impact the future. This usually includes a shedding of obsolete notions and becoming more of who you are at your best.

Your new future is waiting. What might be possible?

---

[4] Dweck, Carol S., Mindset: The New Psychology of Success, Ballantine Books, New York 2008

Patricia Rachel Schwartz

Patricia Rachel Schwartz, MA is passionate about coaching, facilitating, and training leaders and their teams, especially those in transition. She has been active in the field of leadership and management, with businesses and nonprofits in the United States and abroad for 40 years. Her joy is working with those at the forefront of change in their organizations.

Patricia Schwartz delivers trainings, coaching sessions, retreats, and organizational strategic summits. Her strengths-based approach is informed by the latest research in positive psychology. Her methods ignite creativity and innovation. They infuse the organizational culture with positive energy that fosters engagement, resulting in higher productivity. She supports management teams to collaborate effectively in the design and implementation of their future vision. Schwartz's transformational **Relationship Building for Prosperity®** process aligns stakeholders around organizational well-being.

Patricia Schwartz has supported thousands of leaders in corporations, small businesses, higher education, health care, government, entertainment, and nonprofits. It is her greatest honor to be with her clients when they have powerful insights that shift the ground beneath them, leading to unprecedented outcomes for them and their organizations.

Patricia is the principal of her firm Schwartz Associates based in Santa Barbara, CA. She is a senior faculty member of the College of Executive Coaching where she teaches courses and coaches senior leaders. She is also a faculty member of Cal Lutheran University's Center for Nonprofit Leadership. She holds an MA in International Administration and Intercultural Management from the School for International Training in Brattleboro, VT. She is a Professional Certified Coach, Board Certified Coach, and Master Trainer. In her free time, Patricia enjoys volunteer leadership in the community, hiking, cycling, and dancing with her sweetie.

www.PatriciaSchwartz.com
Phone: 805-965-8595
Email: Patricia@PatriciaSchwartz.com
https://www.linkedin.com/in/patriciarachelschwartz
https://www.facebook.com/SchwartzAssociates/
https://twitter.com/PatriciaRSchwar

OUR TIME TO LEAD
BY OLIVIA PARR-RUD, MS

Are you feeling called to step up and share your wisdom? Do you yearn to inspire others? Do you see yourself as a leader? If your answer to any of these questions is "Yes" then I want to say, "Thank you! The world needs you now more than ever."

"Why?" you might ask. "What is different about today?" My answer is one word, "Technology!"

Of course there are many reasons why we need to show up and share our gifts. The world is in a precarious state. Many people express that they feel lost or stressed by daily life and global events. All these issues need our attention. What's different about today? It is because we are globally connected through technology that we are aware of the crises and suffering happening around the world.

So while many of us bemoan the negative aspects of technology, it does have a bright side. Technology offers nearly unlimited opportunities to connect and share with people across the globe. This ease of connectivity has made it possible for more people to connect to a global audience, share their gifts, and inspire or be inspired by others.

Another feature of our advancing technology is an easier entry point for some professions. Consider the field of journalism, for example. Until recently, our main source of information about regional and global events was through centrally-controlled newspapers or radio and television stations. Becoming an internationally known journalist took years of hard work and perhaps a lot of luck. Today, all you need to become a leading journalist is a smart phone, a website, good critical thinking skills, some tech skills, and commitment.

Entertainment is another field that has been revolutionized by technology. Today, we have access to amateur videos from all over the world. And a talented singer/songwriter can quickly become a global star through the clever use of social media.

Each of these examples demonstrates how technology enables us to become leading voices around the world. As we step up and own our roles as influencers and experts, our audiences will see us as leaders. Being seen as a leader offers us great potential to share our gifts and make a positive difference. It also comes with great responsibility. This is especially true for leaders in the corporate world.

Effective Corporate Leadership in the New Paradigm

Fueled by technology and globalization, some large corporations wield immense power. Some companies are more powerful than the largest nation states. And they don't always use their power in positive ways.

As a result, these giant organizations need our positive influence now more than ever. They need us to infiltrate them with love and light. If you like the challenges and opportunities of the corporate world, and like me, are drawn to bringing in love and light, then you need to think of yourself as a leader no matter what position you hold. Why?

Let's look back at a little history. In the early 20th century, most corporate structures were top-down and hierarchical. The CEO was seen as having most of the knowledge. He made the majority of the decisions and gave orders to his subordinates. Managers communicated the orders to the employees. Rarely was anyone's authority questioned or resisted without negative consequences.

Historically, this top-down power structure worked because most jobs were manual or low-tech. So most employees followed the directions of their managers. And markets were more localized and stable over the long term. Because most employees and customers lived in the local community, the culture was an extension of the community. Trust was built on shared goals, values, and interests.

Compare that scenario with business today. Even in the most basic company, virtually everyone needs to know how to use technology. Plus the global markets are constantly changing. So even the best CEO can't possibly know everything or keep up with an ever-evolving business landscape. It just takes too long for the information to go up the chain of command to the CEO for a decision. By the time a CEO's orders get back down to the employees for action, the opportunity has expired. Companies where the CEO makes all the decisions find themselves struggling to compete with more agile competitors.

The companies that are thriving in our fast-paced, high-tech, global economy are the ones that empower all their employees to make important decisions--to think like leaders. They build trust through deep connection and shared goals and values. And this is where you come in. No matter where you are in your work or career, if you step up as a leader you can make a difference.

Steps Towards Effective Leadership

If you decide that you want to show up as a leader in your business or community, let others know through your actions. Why? Because this type of leadership has to be earned.

There are some basic skills and practices that will inspire people to see you as a leader.

- Manage your emotions: Have you ever seen someone get triggered and act out in inappropriately? Can you imagine looking up to that person as a leader? Our first step is to do our own healing work so that we are never defensive or reactive. If we had dysfunctional childhoods, then managing our reactions may be a significant challenge. However, there are many techniques available today for healing trauma and childhood wounds. This personal growth work is essential if we want to be seen and valued as leaders.

- Take an interest in others: Many leaders think they have all the answers. Telling people what to do may work in the short term. But some of the best leaders bring out the wisdom in others. So rather than offering the answers, practice deep listening and allow others to tap into and share their unique wisdom.
- Be curious about the world and question the accepted narrative: As a leader, you can show up as someone who challenges conventional wisdom. You can inspire others by modeling ways to think "out of the box" and offering new perspectives.
- Tap into and listen to your inner guidance: Great leaders know the power of their intuition. Many great CEOs call it "trusting their gut." With the increasing complexity and the volume of information we encounter on a daily basis, it is critical to tap into and trust your own inner guidance.

Actions of Effective Leaders

Taking action is where leadership can be fulfilling. However, it is often where we meet our own resistance. If you are drawn to be a leader but just can't seem to take action, it might help to work with a coach or find friends to inspire and hold you accountable. Once you feel free to move ahead there are many ways you can show up a leader.

- Write: Books and blogs are great ways to share your gifts and step into a thought-leadership role. Writing may even allow you to reach people who seek your services in a more direct leadership role.
- Speak: Local groups are often looking for inspiring speakers. National and international venues are also seeking thought leaders who have ideas for making a positive difference in the world.
- Share: Meetings are a great place to show up as a leader. You can share ideas, acknowledge others, and invite participation from those who are silent. If a business setting isn't available to you, look for local groups where you have an interest and can share your wisdom and inspire others.
- Lead Anywhere: Yes, you can be a leader literally anywhere. You may be in the grocery store checkout line and the person next to you is upset. Rather than feeling annoyed, try feeling some empathy for this person. Your empathy may shift their energy and lead this person to a better feeling place. A simple smile towards someone with a solemn

face can also be an act of leadership. As these people go on to engage with others, all of these actions can have a huge ripple effect.

How to Create an Effective Culture

Once you decide to show up as a leader, you may be invited to lead a group or organization. As you step into this leadership role, the culture that you inspire will determine the ultimate success of your group or organization. There are several foundational characteristics of an effective culture.

- Trust: If you are leading a group or organization, the first step is to create a culture of trust. In today's complex world, the healthiest, most successful groups or teams are those in which everyone contributes. This is only possible when people feel safe to share and contribute without fear of shame or criticism.
- Love: The heart has an energy that allows you to connect deeply with others. If you feel into your heart space and intentionally connect with others, you create a resonance that invites everyone to show up fully and fearlessly.
- Shared Purpose: If you decide to start or join a group, you want to be aligned around a shared purpose. This is often established as the group is forming. As your work progresses, it is valuable to revisit your shared purpose on a regular basis.
- Shared Values: As you step into your role as a leader, work with your team to establish core values. This is best done as a group exercise where everyone participates and feels seen and heard. Shared values are critical to the success of any group endeavor.

Leading Yourself

What you may have noticed is that there isn't a point where you declare yourself a leader. It's really more about allowing yourself to show up as a leader to become the leader that you are. And you can expect that some people will never see you as a leader. And that's okay; they are not your people to lead. If your actions as a leader inspire one or two people, you are making a positive difference in the world. And there may be a ripple effect that is larger than you can imagine. Just focus on what inspires you. Open your heart and share your gifts. Don't be attached to the outcome. Most of all, trust the process and enjoy the journey.

Olivia Parr-Rud, Corporate Love Ambassador

Olivia is a global thought leader, data scientist, and award-winning and best-selling author. Her unique approach to business success draws on her passion for data science, holistic leadership, and personal growth through a blending of left and right brain perspectives. Her latest research unveils the relationship between loving behavior (i.e. compassion, connection, and caring) and long-term corporate profits. Her success with *Data Mining Cookbook* (Wiley 2001) inspired her research in the areas the communication, collaboration, and leadership – highlighted in her second book, *Business Intelligence Success Factors* (Wiley/SAS 2009). In her 4th book, LOVE@WORK, *The Essential Guide to a Life of Inspired Purpose*, Olivia shares her personal story and offers a 4-step method for healing, unveiling and embracing our unique gifts, and stepping into our inspired purpose. Her latest book, *The LOVE@WORK Method*™, *Practices and Tools for Stepping into Your Life of Inspired Purpose* is a practice guide for anyone looking to live a heart-centered life of service to others. She has a Bachelor's of Arts in Mathematics, a Master's of Science in Statistics. Clients include Cisco, Walmart, Wells Fargo, State Farm, HP, IBM, SAS, Xerox, Nationwide, Liberty Mutual, HSBC, Fleet Bank, and Clorox.

www.oliviagroup.com
610 563-8866 (Mobile)
215 948-3500 (Office - message only)
Facebook: https://www.facebook.com/LoveMakeItYourBusiness/

DEVELOPING THE LEADER SELF
BY AERIOL ASCHER

I was so excited to be part of this project and to submit my take on leadership. I pondered for many hours about what leadership meant to me. I consider myself a leader in my field of holistic healing. I consider myself a leader within my business network and entrepreneurial groups. Once I thought about it, it seemed that leadership has been a pretty big part of my life without me being fully conscious of it.

Honestly, **I have always enjoyed leadership roles my whole life.** I moved a lot as a child; I think I went to at least a dozen elementary schools and had the opportunity to re-invent myself over and over again, trying new strategies and approaches to make friends. Once I got a little older I saw leadership as a way that I could meet the most people and be visible to my peers and my teachers. **At a young age, I discovered that you must make yourself visible in order to gain influence in groups.**

I have enjoyed many leadership positions as an adult as well. I have had the opportunity to lead in my music community, in philanthropy groups, in my business networking, in my speaking and coaching business, and in my holistic practice. When I could not identify a group for myself I began just cultivating my own. I never thought twice about it. But still, I had not identified myself as a leader.

I would assume that most people think of a leader as someone with a great deal of education or experience in a certain area. I would even go further to say that there is an implied honorableness, dependableness, and consistency that are required to earn the respect and trust of one's followers. A leader may have a long series of alphabet letters after their name implying fancy educational degrees. They may have important sounding job titles or belong to numerous organizations. These leaders may even contribute their personal time or even their personal finances to the communities they serve.

Obviously, politicians, lawyers, and other officials warrant the title of leader. But isn't a leader more than just a head of state or a government official? Of course! What about teachers? Mentors? Speakers? Spiritual figures? Or how about just mothers? Leadership is something that shapes many different levels of our world. But what makes a good leader?

While knowledge, experience and service are important qualities for a leader, perhaps the absolute number one attribute of an effective leader is their ability to communicate. Without effective communication skills a leader will not be able to inspire their community. Without effective communication skills a leader will not be able to convey their vision. Without effective communication skills a leader will not be able to navigate their professional relationships and see a project or mission through to fruition.

It is easy to understand why the first step in being a good leader is being able to communicate. But what does it *really* take to be a good communicator? Is it having a pleasant voice? Is it studying fancy vocabulary words? I do not think that this is necessarily the case, although all these things certainly improve one's voice and speaking skills.

Don't get me wrong, as a voice and presence coach I share exercises with many of my clients to improve their vocal quality, their tone, and their diction. I believe that these things are all very important and that speaking is a skill that will serve all ambitious leaders to pursue. However, **I also believe that even more important than voice and speaking skills, in order to communicate effectively a good leader must go beyond their voice and presentation skills and first develop a high level of self-awareness.**

As for myself, whether I am working with my healing clients in my holistic practice or voice and presence clients in my coaching business, we start with deep breathing exercises, intention setting, and mindfulness practice to become more self-aware. **These are all the key elements of a healthy self-care practice that lead to greater self-awareness.**

The number one thing voice and presence clients ask me is how to be more confident in front of an audience, the second thing is how to be clearer in their presentation. **Neither one of these things gets in your way once you know your underlying message.** The only way to know your underlying message is to connect with and listen to your inner voice. To do this requires self-awareness.

By developing and cultivating self-awareness a leader can be more successful at identifying their own underlying motivations, managing their emotions, energy, and behaviors. By becoming more self-aware one can begin to navigate more confidently and have more impact in their community. **Self-awareness affords us the luxury of picking clear and precise language to convey our messages in a way that uplifts and inspires others to contribute to a whole.**

Some of the natural bi-products of developing your self-awareness with a daily self-care routine are:

- You will be clear about who you are and aware of your own presence in the world.
- You will strengthen your interpersonal communication skills and learn to listen more effectively.
- You will have the ability to build better rapport with those around you.
- You will increase not only your confidence but also your credibility as a leader.
- You will also be a happier and healthier person.

How is it done? **In order to develop this heightened level of self-assuredness and self-awareness you must commit to examine the whole self at deeper levels.** The "self" as I refer to it is made up of four parts: Physical, Emotional, Mental, and Spiritual. These four aspects make up our whole being or whole self.

Most of us can handle the physical aspect of our self-care routine; we are able to put attention on brushing our teeth, eating right, and getting enough sleep. But it is also important to have a self-care practice that takes into consideration emotional, mental, and spiritual nourishment and fulfillment. Understanding and becoming aware of each of these aspects of Self is the process or practice of Self-Care and it leads to the Self-Awareness that we are talking about.

The more you know yourself and are comfortable with yourself the more you will be able to inspire and motivate those around you to cooperate with you and to accomplish a shared objective and vision. By learning to achieve a relaxed state with a daily self-care practice, you will have more control to access that relaxed and confident state when obstacles or obstructions interrupt your path to success.

In order to maintain the kind of level of self-awareness that affords one confidence and ease it is imperative to develop a routine that includes some sort of mindfulness meditation, prayer, or even yoga to strengthen connection with the self. **Whatever daily practice or relaxation method is employed the important part is commitment and consistency.** Taking time to focus on the breath, clear the mind, listen deeply to the heart, clarify vision, and set intentions that support that vision is all part of a mindfulness practice that supports self-awareness and ultimately communication.

This kind of Self-Awareness through Self-Care and Personal Development is the foundation of excellence in your life and excellence as a communicator and leader. After all, before you can inspire others, you must first understand your own motivations, behaviors, and emotions. For continued and sustained success you must develop and maintain a routine or protocol that supports the heightened awareness that you have about all the aspects of your whole self and of truly loving yourself.

Part of knowing oneself and taking responsibility for one's life is by developing a life vision. Who do you want to be? How do you want to live? How does it feel when you do? These are important aspects that you need to examine on your path to awareness. A daily self-care practice including mindfulness meditation can help with this by learning to listen to your inner voice and examining your values and dreams.

It is important to reach deeply inside and uncover your passion and your purpose. How does this shape and motivate your life vision? The more you know yourself the more you will begin to trust yourself to go in a direction that supports your vision. Once you truly gain your own trust you will never compromise your beliefs or values to achieve a goal or for other temporary gain.

By learning to know and respect yourself you will be able to keep in mind your own limitations and flaws and be able to realistically move towards goals by recruiting others that compliment your skill sets. You will also learn to build healthy boundaries by knowing your needs and expectations of yourself and others. You can stay energized by taking the time to learn what activities re-energize you and which ones drain your energy. With a little mindfulness and planning you will be able to keep your energy fully recharged, so you can always give your best effort.

Once you have put your attention on your relationship with yourself and you have developed a strong sense of who you are and what you are up to in the world you need to look at your level of commitment to that relationship with yourself. This requires that you strengthen your inner discipline and learn self-management. Learning to take responsibility for your behavior, attitudes, and actions can raise your performance level as well as help you to build trust with others.

Do not be afraid to seek the input of others. Check in with people, follow up with people, and listen to what feedback they make. Ask people how you are doing at communicating your vision and then hold yourself accountable for your actions and performance. Right any wrongs as they come up and keep moving ahead.

Take initiative to delegate responsibilities and tasks. Remember that it is your job as a leader to lead. Find team members who have complimentary skill sets so you can collaborate. Always take care to avoid micromanaging your team. Instead have a clear and articulate picture of what you want and allow the other person to do what they say they are going to do.

It is important that you be *confident enough in yourself to surround yourself with talented, qualified people on your team*. *The people you are surrounded by are a reflection of your work and your world.* **Choose amazing people to be around who share your vision and values.**

On the subject of the people in your community, **it is also important as a leader and communicator that you develop your social awareness.** Show genuine concern for others and learn how to actively listen. Don't just wait for your turn to speak, but listen intently to the other person and respond only when they are finished speaking. Doing so will build rapport and create lasting bonds and a strong community.

Give others a reason to support you and your vision. **Be someone that they want to be around. Be generous not only in spirit but be generous with your words to uplift those around you.** Let others know when they have done a good job and look for ways to openly recognize and reward excellence. By doing this you will build a culture of praise and acknowledgement in your community.

Help others to increase their abilities and fully utilize their talents by providing opportunities for training and self-development. Mentor others to lead. You will never lose when you take a stance to empower others. **Learn how to bring out the best in yourself and others. Utilize everyone's best qualities and minimize their limitations with effective assignment of tasks and delegation of responsibilities no matter how big or small.** In other words, don't expect your best creative artist-type friend to be a great fit to be the CFO of your organization!

Regardless of your education or experience, you can achieve greater success as a leader by learning how to use your communication and people skills to fully harness the talents and energy of others. These strategies will allow you to increase your confidence and certainty, up your self-care game and inspire others to fully enlist in your project or cause of their own free will. You will never feel uncomfortable or at a loss for words when asked to introduce yourself or explain a project. You will naturally begin to magnetize your community.

Doesn't it feel better to attract your people rather than to try to convince people to enlist in your cause? Doesn't it feel better not to have to push, to prove, to compete? And it is easy, isn't it? When you develop self-awareness and a whole self-care routine to support a clear mind, clear vision, and souring spirit—when you can shine your light fully and authentically, non-apologetically—those who you are meant to lead will appear. Are you ready? It's time for you to lead like the leader that you are.

Leadership Development Tips:

1. Develop strong self-care practices.
2. Spend time each day truly connecting with yourself, your values, purpose, and vision.
3. Communicate your truth, vision, and purpose clearly.
4. Become self-aware. Discover your strengths and weaknesses.

5. Delegate! Surround yourself with great people and delegate according to their strengths.
6. Be a leader people want to be around.
7. Step fully into your authentic, self-aware leadership self...and SHINE!

Aeriol Ascher

Aeriol Ascher is an Author, Speaker, Podcast Personality, Holistic Entrepreneur, Teacher, Mentor, and Coach. She holds a Bachelor's Degree in Theatre Arts from Santa Clara University, a Master's of Religious Science and a Doctor of Metaphysics Degree with the Universal Life Church. She has collected numerous holistic healing certifications.

Aeriol is a leader in the field of holistic self-care, personal development, and transformation. Her business gained recognition in 2009 when her signature energy healing service was named Best Massage in Silicon Valley by the San Jose Mercury News. She earned the title three more times before her holistic healing center Reiki Angel Intuitive Arts landed the title or Best Day Spa in Silicon Valley in 2015.

She empowers clients and audiences with tools they can immediately employ to powerfully and confidently show up, speak up, and stand out in their personal and professional lives. Her clients learn how to energize their body, clear their mind, harness the power of their intentions and most importantly awaken the magic of the voice with mindfulness meditation and a daily practice of radical self-care.

Aeriol is available for speaking engagements, trainings, coaching, and personal healing retreats in the San Francisco Bay Area or via video conferencing technology. Aeriol's Whole Self Care podcast entitled "Healing Body Mind and Soul with Aeriol" is available on iTunes.

Learn More about Aeriol's Coaching Business: www.AeriolAscher.com

Aeriol's Private Healing Practice: www.SomaSoundTherapy.com

Tune into Aeriol's Podcast: www.HealingBodyMindandSoul.com

Social Links:
www.facebook.com/askaeriol
www.facebook.com/somasoundtherapy
www.instagram.com/askaeriol/
www.twitter.com/askaeriol
www.youtube.com/user/ReikiAngelMassage
www.linkedin.com/in/aeriolascher/

IT'S NOT A SOLO JOURNEY
EVERY EXPERT NEEDS EXPERTS
BY KATHLEEN SIMS

I have been living in the question, "What is an Expert?" It seems to me an Expert is a person who has mastered a specialty. The second question that naturally comes out of that is, "How does one become an Expert?" What I have seen in my own process is we don't become an Expert by traveling a solo journey. There are certain phases a person goes through in learning and growth before they are elevated to the level of being seen as an Expert with a specialty. Mastery takes innate talent and a committed interest in a specific subject along with challenging personal experiences in which growth and breakthroughs occur, study, research, learning, and teaching. . . and an ability to communicate inspiringly and clearly about the subject. It usually is an ongoing, lifetime developmental process. I couldn't have made it successfully to be known as a Source for learning in certain specialties without drawing on Experts along the way in areas I am not fluent in. **What I have seen in my own process is we don't become an Expert by traveling a solo journey**.

I am considered an Expert on Love, Empowerment, and Life Purpose. I ask myself, "How did I attain this level of recognition?" I see that each of these subjects has had a life of its own filled with challenges, growth, and learning simultaneously.

Journey to Love

My process of becoming a Love Expert came out of several things that really impacted me. First, manifesting my Soulmate, Jim, at age 16, then taking 15 years to do research and study to figure out how that had happened to me. Add in 40 years of being in a special, loving relationship that was also filled with very difficult issues that came up that we had to resolve and learn from them. Each situation demanded hard work from both of us, calling on Mentors and Experts to help us see our blind spots, learning new methods to resolve issues, healing historical blocks, and growth work. Along the way we took some relationship courses and went to couples counseling when needed. I experienced such a deepening of understanding about relating, connecting, and loving. I didn't know love could feel like this given what I observed about my unhappy parents. Jim and I adored and admired each other, had mutual respect, trust, laughed and loved a lot. I remember my husband once saying, "Kath, you are precious and I know you to the marrow of your bones," I felt seen and accepted. One morning my husband passed me in the hall and reached over to hug me, however, he didn't just hug me—he held me—and he said in my ear, **"I don't know anyone who has the kind of love we have, and everyone deserves it." This ignited in me an even stronger commitment to reach more people with my Love Teachings,** which also expanded my knowledge and understanding in the process. The more we grew and learned, the deeper our connection became, and the more our love blossomed into amazing mature love.

While teaching and counseling singles and couples, I challenged myself to learn as much as possible. I saw clients half time in my Practice and I went to work half time for a singles organization (before online dating). The project I took on was interviewing 1,000 single people desiring to have a love relationship. I helped them clarify their vision for that ideal love relationship. Then we uncovered what were the obstacles that stood in the way of them having this in their past. I gave everyone personality assessments and researched the qualities that made a couple easily compatible, raising the potential for a successful, lasting love relationship.

The knowledge I derived from doing this research project and using this personality assessment not only deepened my understanding of relationships, which helped empower my clients, it also transformed some key issues with my husband and me.

A few years later is when people started doing online dating, which was somewhat like a computer version of the work I had been doing at the singles organization. My commitment to my work with clients is to only coach clients in areas I have personally experienced and researched. At that particular time, I had four clients wanting me to coach them in effective online dating. It had been a couple of years since I lost my husband of 40 years to a sudden heart attack. I didn't feel ready for a serious relationship; however, I had been missing having men friends in my life and socializing, so I decided I would take on a new research project: how to safely and effectively do online dating. So I rolled up my sleeves and started the process of online dating, trying different sites with a variety of demographics, creating protocols for safety, and questions for vetting. Little did I know how much I would learn about the vetting, first meeting, matching and dating process, along with discovering new things about myself and men. (Remember, I got married in high school, so I had never dated as an adult.) I interfaced with about 200 men, and met in person about 60. I had some dull and some amazing experiences—a very broad spectrum that I could write a very juicy book about. That was 15 years ago. A few of those men are still good friends of mine. Also, low and behold, and much to my surprise, in that process I met my second Soulmate, Bob. We had an amazing deep connection even before we spoke. The first time we met in a restaurant, he hugged me and I felt a déjà vu feeling in the core of my body as if we had been together before in a past life. He was an adventurous Soul and we starting having the time of our lives.

Journey to Empowerment

Empowerment was what I yearned for as a child but not what I experienced. I have a distinct memory at age six of meeting my first grade teacher. She was so kind and loving. I thought I'm going to be a mom and teacher just like her. Then at twelve I was sent to a social worker to get help in dealing with my violent father. It was a horrible experience. She was not only not helpful, she made me very uncomfortable. On the way home from one of those sessions I remember thinking: *"Isn't there counseling offered that actually helps people?"* **Right then and there I made a decision that when I grow up I'm going to be a counselor and teacher, so children have more loving parents and live a better childhood than I had.** I felt a deep sense of a Calling, having no idea how to make that dream come true.

I remember my father encouraging my brother to go to college; however, supporting a girl to go to college to him seemed like a waste of money. "After all," he would say, "girls just grow up and get married and become housewives, and then all that money is wasted." He would tell me, "Become a secretary, then you can marry the boss who went to college and is making a lot of money."

Given that kind of upbringing, needless to say, it embedded a deep concern about having children and wanting to raise them differently...but how? I remember as a young mother reflecting very seriously on what was helpful and what was harmful to me in my childhood. I drew on the helpful things but saw there were a lot of blind spots and missing pieces to the puzzle of conscious parenting. When my children were six and eight, the younger one started getting stomachaches from going to school. I was desperate to find something that would help her. I needed an Expert. After seeing a medical doctor and a counselor, it was decided that her home environment was very comfortable making the difference a big gap when she was in a school room with all the chaos and pressure. The counselor said send her to school anyway, so she would press through her fears, rather than coddle her at home embedding even more that she was only safe at home, away from school. It was so hard for me to have her be so uncomfortable. An amazing thing happened. In about a week and a half her stomachaches went away and she was growing more comfortable about being at school.

This left me in a quandary. Was making my home comfortable a bad thing? Yikes. I didn't know where to find a helpful Expert on parenting. I stumbled upon a Conscious Parenting class, feeling a dire need to learn some new parenting techniques. I gained tools to become an empowering parent.

I learned from Margo, the teacher, that being a Conscious Parent and empowering our children was seeing them as whole and complete, and supporting them with empowering questions that lead to self discovery, learning to think for themselves, and trust themselves. Very different than giving advice and trying to control outcomes. I learned how essential it is to provide a safe place for someone to learn and discover answers within themselves. They have to feel safe enough to make a journey of inquiry by knowing it's ok to get it wrong or make a mistake. If we're afraid of being wrong or making a mistake the discovery process gets blocked. This leads to a natural path of finding solutions right for that person. What I have grown to cherish using this empowering technique is that it doesn't give answers, rather it helps people discover knowledge they didn't realize they possessed. Very empowering.

I also learned how essential it is to heal the wiring in the brain caused from traumas, upsetting past incidents, and negative beliefs about one's self and life. We can make fundamental changes if the subconscious dysfunctions are transformed. As time goes on more technologies are discovered for healers and psychologists to use in helping clients be free. In my search I learned from many amazing Experts. The additional wonderful thing about these ways of healing and exploring, both for children and adults, is that it impacts one's self esteem in a positive way to realize we can heal emotionally and mentally, along with tapping into our inner guidance and finding our own answers, which is priceless.

Looking back at what I went through in my childhood, and what a lot of others have gone through, and making this available for parents and children, and the inner child of the parent, brings me to tears. Healing through generations can happen and transform our world.

Journey to Life Purpose

Remember my first Mentor, Margo, the Conscious Parenting teacher? She said to me, "If I had a child, I would put them into this transformational training for children." My daughter was back in school; however, she still needed some confidence building experiences. So I called the training company to enroll her and they said a child could only take the training if they had one parent who had done their transformational training for adults. I had no idea what it was; however, I was very motivated to have my daughter do the training, so I signed up. Yikes! I had never done any growth work except that parenting class. I had no idea what I was getting into.

An amazing thing happened during that weekend. I had a transformational experience of resurrecting the yearning I had when I was six years old, then again at twelve years old, of being a teacher and counselor, helping parents to be the best they could be, and helping to heal adults of their childhood traumas. A dream I had let go of years prior because I married so young and became a teen mom. In addition, remember my father's discouraging words about the idea of me going to college. All this had added up to my childhood dreams becoming faded memories.

In this training the remembrance of my Calling activated my deep desire to counsel, heal, and teach others, and brought with it an insight from "On High": "You can do it and you can do it your way!" (Not the way the outside world says you are supposed to do it.)

I did challenging personal growth work—both inner and outer transformations—followed guidance and had breakthroughs along the way. I went through a major metamorphosis. I lost 40 pounds without dieting. It felt like for the first time in my life I was reflecting on the outside who I knew myself to be on the inside. Within about six months I landed my dream job. And of all things I became a teacher and counselor, with on-the-job training from Mentors and Experts within the organization—no college necessary.

I was blessed to have my dream job for ten wonderful years: traveling around the country, teaching transformational Personal Power Seminars to thousands of women, training other trainers, developing advanced workshops, and serving on the Management Team during a successful business turn around. I experienced making a true contribution–very fulfilling. My prayers were answered and my Calling Manifest.

And then in a major management change, the organization changed their philosophy and values; I saw it was time to leave. I was complete; however, I had no idea what to do next. I went through a lot of deep inquiry and a dark night of the Soul in which I had to confront and re-evaluate every value I held dear. I was fearful I'd never be able to do My Calling any more. How could this be? I started to pray without ceasing. *"Please God, use me. Show me the way. What do I do? Where can I make the best contribution given my gifts and these circumstances?"*

Then it happened! In a blink of an eye, the Heavens opened up. An epiphany that changed my life forever. I saw a picture and a message that was profound: the earth with triangles of Light covering it completely and that Light radiating everywhere. I heard: *"This is the Perfection of the Divine Plan made manifest. Everyone has their Part in the Whole. That also means You!"*

Each "Point of Light" represented people all around the planet. There was a place for everyone to share the gifts they had been given from "On High." In so doing, every need on the planet was met, and harmony and peace prevailed.

I got out my journal and began to write. The information was coming through me as fast as I could capture it: *"These are the Steps one must go through to realize at a cellular level this same Divine Truth for themselves."*

When I was done writing I looked at what had been written. It was a three-day Spiritual Intensive called "Live Your Vision."

More words were flowing through me as fast as I could write. My Life Purpose revealed itself: *To celebrate the preciousness of this Joyous Dance of Life, embracing myself and others in God's Perfect Love, freeing our Spirits to soar as One.*

Every cell of my Being was vibrating at a speed I wasn't accustomed to. I read everything I wrote and began to sob. I couldn't stop. I knew I was not the same person who had been lying there just one hour before and for these many long months.

"Now what? No one will hire me to do this," I thought. And I had never wanted to own my own business. So what on earth was I supposed to do with this information and insight?

I was told, *"Get out of bed, get dressed and talk to anyone who will listen."* **I realized that my biggest challenge now was to have faith and courage.** I followed the instructions, opened my heart, and began sharing my profound insights and passion about these Divine Truths.

Before I knew it, a business had organically taken form around me: The Center for Conscious Living. I was teaching "Live Your Vision" in businesses, transforming their culture, and teaching it to the public, transforming individuals' lives, coaching, and doing healing work. I loved what I was doing even more than I had loved my old training job. This really was me Living My Vision!

I created a Consortium of healers and counselors at The Center; however, I only needed to be there part time which served my lifestyle given I was also raising my grandson at the time. For ten years I was satisfied with this level of success. I contemplated expanding my business at that point, however, I didn't know how to do that. So I hired a friend who was an Expert at marketing and sales strategies. She coached me for a few months, making some progress. Then out of the blue my husband, Jim, passed away suddenly of a heart attack. He had been healthy and had just turned 60. We had been together since I was sixteen. Talk about a shock on every level. Threw me into grief and an identity crisis. Not to mention in my face was the fact that I had been working my business as a part-time endeavor.

Not taking myself fully seriously as a business owner. (After Jim's passing our household income instantly went down by 75%! Talk about a rude awakening.) Because of the circumstances, Anne, my dear friend, the Marketing Expert – whom I had known for twenty years and who had known my husband – stepped forward and pledged to coach me as a gift with the goal of doubling my business in a year so I could continue sharing My Calling, and actually support myself and my grandson. With Anne's generous gift and support we surpassed the goal. My Practice had become full time. Yeah! Now it was time to get a Visibility Coach. An arena I didn't know much about. Rebecca Hall Gruyter came into my life. She created opportunities in which I was able to give motivational talks to spread the word, co-authoring several books, and expanding my audience to teach about Love, Empowerment, and Life Purpose.

I've now been on this path for thirty years and I find it valuable to look back and reflect and ask myself how did all this manifest? It certainly came from a lot of hard work, messages from "On High" helping me, and following the clues that showed up along the way. I surpassed my wildest dreams of loving what I do, fulfilling my Life Purpose, and making a contribution to the world spreading Love and Light.

What stands out to me as I look back are all the Experts and Mentors who have helped me on my journey. No, I didn't get my degree; however, I did get in touch with my innate gifts and developed them. I have had so many wonderful teachers and Mentors. I would re-evaluate where I was each year and uncover what my next undeveloped part of myself was needing an upgrade. Then I found a teacher/Expert in that arena and learned from them. **The truth is that we are not good at everything that is needed to succeed in a business. Learn and develop what is possible, and delegate what isn't.** I feel like I got thirty years of an amazing education—with trials and errors along the way. My list of contributors to my success is pages long. They blessed me with their knowledge and influenced me powerfully in my Awakening. Even if you are an entrepreneur, you don't succeed alone on an island!

Life is not a solo journey. Look for Mentors and Experts to let into your life so you can fully step into your power and manifest your destiny. Remember the world is waiting and needs You— your light, your love, your gifts and talents.

Expert Tips:

1. Be willing to tell your Truth about your deepest dreams and your Calling.
2. Share your dream with everyone you meet.
3. Identify the areas in which you need support.
4. Find the perfectly matched Experts that can mentor you to grow to that next level.
5. Become and share the One you came here to be, making a difference that fills your heart.

Kathleen Sims

Kathleen E. Sims, D.D., C.H.T., is Co-Founder of The Center for Conscious Living in Pleasant Hill, CA, and CEO of Certain Solutions, a Visionary Management Consulting Firm, *teaching Universal Principles in corporations, activating culture transformations.*

Graduate of the University of Science and Philosophy, and Certified as a Life Coach from J.F.K. and The Relationship Coaching Institute, Kathleen has taught at J.F.K. University and served on the Board in their Transformation in Business MBA Program.

Serving clients globally, she is known as Kathleen The Love Coach, bringing her "Body of Work" forth in many forms: Soul-based counseling, spiritual healing, hypnotherapy, EMDR, brainspotting, life and love coaching, and transformational workshops. Her work is mystical, yet practical, based on Universal Spiritual Principles and Transformational Coaching Technologies, resulting in permanent change.

Kathleen is gifted with the unique ability to draw from deep personal experiences and tap into Truths from "On High," translating them into The Legacy of Love Teachings, so others can attract deep abiding Love also. Having had two Soulmates, she's cracked the code on Soulmate relationships and empowering women to create a life they truly love, with the love of their life by their side.

Co-authoring six personal growth books that have hit #1 led to an interview on Voice America Radio, TV and an article in RHG Magazine, sharing her inspiring Love Story. She's spreading more love in the world through her YouTube Channel and her soon to be released book, *Evolutionary Love - Creating and Sustaining Everlasting Soulmate Love.*

Full Name: **Kathleen E. Sims, C.H.T., C.R.C.**
Email: kathleen@kathleenthelovecoach.com
Phone Number: **925 914-0098** or **925 674-9003**
Website: **Kathleenthelovecoach.com**
Facebook:
Professional Page: Kathleen - Love Coach
www.facebook.com/kathleenthelovecoach/
Personal Page: Kathleen E. Sims
https://www.facebook.com/kathleen.e.sims
Twitter: **https://twitter.com/2melifesadance**
LinkedIn:
https://www.linkedin.com/in/
kathleen-e-sims-a879259?trk=nav_responsive_tab_profile_pic
YouTube Channel:
https://www.youtube.com/user/KathleentheLoveCoach

SECTION 3:

Your Leadership in Action

VISION AND COMMITMENT,
TWO IMPORTANT INGREDIENTS OF LEADERSHIP
BY PASTOR NICOLAS C PACHECO

Leadership is meant to inspire others to discover their strengths and weaknesses and thereby be able to generate a vision that gives direction and meaning.

Throughout our lives we have crossed paths with people with a lot of potential who speak to us, encourage us, make us see the reality of things. However, not everyone manages to awaken in us an interest in learning more or creating the impulse to act.

We all possess qualities and skills that while unique to us are also enviable to others. We also have experiences and past emotions that push us or hinder us from making decisions with the potential to impact our lives one way or another. Therefore, our past, especially our childhood, plays a very important role. If someone had a toxic childhood where he was repressed or pointed out as inferior to others, it will probably lead to difficulty when making tough decisions or facing adversity. On the other hand, if someone had a healthy childhood and grew up to have a secure sense of self and is comfortable in his identity he will be more capable of dealing with difficult situations and will stand out as having the potential for being a great leader.

People who are secure in themselves are more likely to be thrust into positions of leadership. Those who have faced obstacles in their lives and have emerged victorious are especially fit for these positions. In fact, adversities are excellent for strength and character building. It is well known that those with the potential to be great leaders do not have a common denominator, meaning that their social position, race, and gender are not what is driving them; even things like political party or tastes in food and music are not contributing factors. **Leaders are shown by how they have handled adversities and opportunities that have appeared in their lives.**

By examining leaders' lives we often find words like *Perseverance, Attitude, Humility, Courage, Vision,* and *Commitment* when they speak of how they got to where they are today. Here we'll be looking at two important aspects of leadership: Vision and Commitment.

VISION

Carl Jung said, "Whoever looks outside, dreams; who looks inside, awakes." **It is important to look in and out to have vision.** By examining our interior, we can gain enough knowledge to recognize skills and weaknesses, fears, hidden dreams, frustrated goals. When we examine our outside, we realize that there is a world full of possibilities and challenges to overcome. We realize that every day is an opportunity to improve and open new horizons. Every time we reach a goal, we realize that it is only a step on a path that does not end until our last breath.

As we walk, we fall, we grow, we advance, and something precious happens—our character is formed. In this continuous awakening we realize that many past experiences, although at the time painful, were to our benefit. Character formation not only changes who we are inside, but it also makes us see life in a different way. Life changes when we change ourselves. It is very important that we do not evaluate our past decisions based on our knowledge today as we would more than likely drown in regret and second guess our future decisions.

Our decisions reflect the desires of our heart. Our heart harbors desires that manifest themselves in conscious and unconscious behaviors. Our reaction to certain events reflects what we really want. Between where we are and where we want to be we have created an imaginary route—it is our vision. **Without that gap it is not possible to start walking in the right direction.**

What do you want? Where do you want to see yourself in the next five years? What makes you sing? What makes you dream? What makes you cry? What makes you laugh? These are some of the most significant questions for the individual; they will decide your direction, your effort, your courage and your patience. If you do not see much in the distance, it is important that you go up one more step; it will surely give you a better angle of the promised land. Who inspires you? Who would you like to follow the steps? Why? With whom would you like to walk this journey? Is there someone you would like to see with you in this new adventure?

If you suddenly ask yourself why you do not have a vision like the others, let me ask you: is there something that prevents you? Do you carry a burden that hinders you? Is there something that does not let you be authentic? Is there someone you can trust and ask for advice? Remember that in solitude it is very easy to convince yourself of anything, that is why it is dangerous and, in many cases, not recommended. Do not be wise in your own opinion, look for someone you can trust and help show you what cannot see.

Many times, we confuse loneliness with isolation. Loneliness is that time alone that every human being needs to have, that moment where the leader reflects, puts his thoughts in order, evaluates the way traveled and the way to walk; that time is not only necessary but precious and healthy. Loneliness is putting your distractions in a cage. On the other hand, isolation is negative and toxic; it is when you put yourself in a cage. It's not because you want to be alone some time, but you do not want to be with anyone. This not only limits your learning and understanding of reality, but it makes you believe in your own reality. A vision taking isolation as a companion is not a realistic vision. **Remember, dreams are not enemies of reality, fantasies are. When we forge a vision in the middle of isolation it is very likely that we are not forming a dream, but rather a fantasy.**

A toxic childhood or a past with destructive experiences can create a sense of uncertain future or a future that we do not deserve because of our past. It is important to heal the soul first. Many people cannot dream big or generate a vision in their lives, because they still believe all the negativity that they were told many years ago. We cannot put aged wine in broken bottles. It is important to heal inside and then have a clear vision. From the abundance of positive matter in our hearts, no doubt words will come out full of encouragement, faith, and hope.

To have a vision it is important to be honest with ourselves. Everything you do has to coincide with your values, your beliefs, and your morals, that is, with what is important, what is true, and what is correct. If what you are seeing for yourself in the future does not fit with these three elements, it is better to wait before deciding. Many times, we plan to build on loose ground, with doubts and uncertainty. In those moments, when our inner voice tells us that something is not right it is better to wait and seek wise advice, and prepare a solid ground that allows us to ensure the best scenario for success. Delaying is not a good friend for many of us, but when it is used wisely, that is precisely where the best projects come from.

If you are working on projects and you already have a concrete vision, then now is the time to start walking and give shape, life to that project, and to make a commitment.

COMMITMENT

It is very likely that many of us have started something without commitment, perhaps by chance, coincidence, or even by mistake. It is possible to start without commitment, but it is nearly impossible to continue or finish without it. **Commitment is a necessary ingredient to be able to cross the line of success.**

When opportunities arise, it is important to see if they fit with the vision that you have in mind for yourself. If the shoe fits, then take advantage of it and make a solid commitment and use it to further your vision. If it is does not fit in with your vision, then ignore it as it can be a distraction with great consequences; it can steal your time, your talents, or your treasures and will not benefit you but only delay you. **Remember that we do not get the things we want but the ones that we focus on.**

Do not make commitments that you won't be able to fulfill. It is important to know what our skills are and what our limits are—that will give us freedom to make promises and be able to keep them. There is time to prepare; remember, when the opportunity arrives it is too late to prepare. Staying in continuous training will not only make us better at what we are good at, but it will also make us grow in new areas and discover skills we did not know about. The great leaders discovered skills just when they were walking into a project; the same need and survival instinct makes us look where we do not believe there is. Remember, treasures are not always found under rocks, but when it happens it is always a surprise.

Once you have detected an opportunity and recognized that you can do it, that is the time to take responsibility and walk in the direction of the vision and make the commitment to finish. What starts well ends well. Even when things do not come out completely as one wishes, it is sure to leave us with a sense of satisfaction of having tried. But if it was a success, it leaves a standard of doing things correctly. Even when you try and fail there is an apprenticeship. As John Maxwell says: "Sometimes you win and sometimes you learn."

Vision and commitment go hand in hand. They are the heart and the head; we need both. Your vision will not be fulfilled without a commit-ment. A commitment without vision will be like when Alice in Wonderland meets the cat at the crossroads. Alice asks which path she should take, and the cat tells her that it depends on where she wants to go, to which she replies that she does not know. The cat finally tells her, then take any path, it's the same, it does not matter.

What is your vision? Do you already have it? Are you willing to take responsibility and give life to that dream? Make a commitment, stick to it, give it your all, and always act with faith. Put all these factors together and you have the recipe for a great potential success or a learning experience.

Vision and Commitment Tips:

1. What do you want? What is your dream?
2. What skills do you have to support this dream?
3. What steps need to be taken to bring this dream forward?
4. Are you willing to take the steps to see this dream through to completion?
5. If yes, then commit and start taking steps to lead your dream into reality.

Nicolas C. Pacheco

Nicolas C. Pacheco is a church planter in the San Francisco Bay Area. He is a graduate of the Gateway Seminary, formerly known as Golden Gate Baptist Theological Seminary. He is a PREPARE & ENRICH facilitator, and founder of "Destruyendo Barreras," a marriage restoration ministry. He is also an independent certified coach, teacher, and speaker for the John Maxwell Team. Pastor Pacheco is also a certified Life Coach, Life Impact LLC. As of 2017 Pastor Pacheco was recruited to teach at California Crosspoint Academy; he teaches both middle and high school students Spanish and Bible Studies. Also, in 2017 he began coaching at Cardinal Education. He currently serves as director of the Hispanic extension of the seminary, CLD, and as Pastor of Iglesia Bautista Dulce Refugio in Oakland, CA. Recently, Pastor Pacheco attended a professional development program and received a certification for Leadership Coaching Strategies at Harvard University. He is also a co-author of the Amazon bestseller anthology, *Empowering You, Transforming Lives: Daily Inspiration to Help You Live On Purpose and with Purpose*, published on December 4, 2018.

pastornpacheco@nicolascpacheco.com
nicolaspacheco244@gmail.com
510-228-7255
www.nicolascpacheco.com
www.linkedin.com/in/nicolascpacheco
http://www.johnmaxwellgroup.com/nicolascpacheco
YouTube: Nicolas C Pacheco

THE LEADERS' SECRET WEAPON
WAIT FOR IT...IT'S A GIFT
BY JEANNE ALFORD

We are a distracted society.

There. I said it.

Let's start with how we are inundated. In the 1990s, one daily newspaper had the amount of information that a man in the 17th century would have gathered in a year. Yes, a year! That factoid was given before social media existed. We were still figuring out the World Wide Web back then. To take this further, a study by the University of California San Diego indicates that the average American's daily media information consumption reached 34 gigabytes. 34. That's a doable number, right? No! That's the equivalent of a Stephen King novel PLUS several hours of video every day. Before you wipe your brow and say, "Whoa," consider this: that study was done in 2009, when Facebook and Twitter were in their infancy.

As a leader, why do we care how much information we consume? Simply put, distraction.

Another key study done by Siemens shows that employees spend nearly 17.5 hours a week addressing miscommunications. For a small business with 100 employees, that's a productivity loss of more than a half million dollars a year. Consider how many conversations you have in a day. Now add emails, reports, memos, phone calls, texts, social media updates, and popular group notification programs like Asana and Slack. That can add up to a huge amount of miscommunication opportunities.

It's this realization that leads me to discuss a leader's super powers. I identify these as **BCL: Breathe Choose Listen.**

- **Breathe.** I'm a proponent of taking a deep breath. Breathing is a skill we learned in our infancy and don't pay too much attention to. A good muscle-memory skill, it keeps us alive. The simple act of taking a deep breath signals your brain that you are not in danger, thus moving your thinking from the fight-flight-freeze realm of the amygdala to the more logical frontal lobe. In other words, it gives your brain time to catch up before you open your mouth, something that today's leaders are learning is clearly an important power.
- **Choose.** Choice is a critical skill and allows us to control our personal world. Often overlooked as a skill, choice is one of those things that can put you in heaven – a space of acceptance and control – or hell – a space of chaos and stress. I don't know about you, but I prefer the former. When you consciously practice choice, you make the decision to react emotionally or respond thoughtfully and deliberately. I often say it's between the stimulus and the response when you choose whether you live in heaven or hell. Leaders who practice this skill love living in heaven.
- **Listening.** The amount of distraction, activity, or noise we face every day makes it difficult to give everything the necessary attention. Another study, published in ADWEEK, focused on social media alone. This study showed the average adult is exposed to 285 pieces of content every day. This translates to 54,000 words, 1,000 clicks and 7 hours of video. That's social media alone. It's estimated that the workforce spends 2.3 hours a day on social media which only adds to the level of distractions we face daily. It's a wonder that we can even think clearly, let alone listen, but that's a choice! To listen.

I call listening a super power. Why? It's a *gift* to hear what we say to each other. It's a gift to give your conversation partner your full attention.

I had the great pleasure to work with one of the founders of what we know as Silicon Valley, Robert "Bob" Noyce. When I met him, he was CEO at Intel, was active in working with President Reagan and about 35 bipartisan congressmen, and so much more on his plate. He was, in my book, a rock star.

I worked at an association and he was on our Board of Directors. One day I needed to get his attention and asked him for information for a reporter on deadline. Bob, who was just leaving a meeting, stopped. I remember he looked me in the eye and said, "I would love to hear more about this. Walk with me." We discussed the issue and he gave me two response options. Then he took my breath away. He said, "Let me know if they need to get me on the phone. I'll make time for you. Thank you, you are doing a great job." Frankly, until that moment, I didn't know he even knew my name! He modeled for me how a leader takes whatever time needed to stop, listen, and choose how to respond. He also showed me how a leader, with very little effort, empowers people to do what they do best.

Let me ask, do you listen? Of course you do. Right? Or not.

Most of us think we are listening. However, it's simply human nature to interrupt our listening brain with thoughts of how we are going to respond. We worry about what we can say to impress our conversation partner. We plot how we are going to show them our wit and wisdom. It becomes the driving thought pattern and is so strong that we are not even aware that we didn't hear the "rest of the story," as journalist Paul Harvey would say.

Think about this. You are on the panel for Family Feud with Steve Harvey. You're at the buzzer, primed to win the round. Steve, in his dramatic voice, says, "According to 100 women surveyed, the best room in the house to...."

Bam!

You hit the buzzer. What are you going to answer? The best room in the house to what? Eat lunch? Clean the kids' toy box? Talk to your spouse? Do your work? The possibilities are endless.

You hit the buzzer. You must answer. You take a wild guess and say, "The kitchen." You know your chances of winning the round have just plummeted. Steve gives you that signature "What Were You Thinking" glare, then repeats the question: "According to 100 women surveyed, the best room in the house to hide packages is..." and you look at the board. Your answer was there but it was Number 5. You just gave your opponent an opening.

It's at this point that we need to get stronger at interrupting our internal interrupter. In this example, a simple five seconds would have made a world of difference.

Using this as an illustration, think about how often you find yourself interrupting your listening brain. I know I catch myself regularly. I admit this even though I've practiced the skill for a long time. It is so ingrained in us that it may be part of the survival mechanism we all are born with.

Not hearing the whole question in the Family Feud example, or not hearing the full opinion in our daily conversations, is the genesis of most misunderstandings. We miss out on critical information. Think of how many hours we can save if we simply listened and understood each other. When we communicate, I advocate knowing what you want to say, who you are talking to and why it would be important to them and what you want them to do. When listening, we need to be sure we understand what the speaker wants us to know, why they think we care and what they want. Is that hard? **Well, if the workforce is spending, on average, 17.5 hours a week trying to figure it out, I'd say it's paramount to know what to listen for and to actively repeat it, so we can be certain what's important.**

Since we believe we listen to each other every day, listening may be one of the more difficult super powers to improve. Therefore, today's leaders stand out when they apply it to their daily activities. More important, by practicing active and effective listening, leaders and experts model a new behavior that others will strive to emulate.

But what do I mean by actively listening?

Attention:

Let's start with giving the speaker attention. Bob Noyce did that for me when he stopped and looked me in the eye before he responded.

Actively hearing what the speaker is saying may not be as easy as it sounds, as demonstrated earlier. It's important to make it clear you are giving 100% of your attention. You need to provide verbal and non-verbal cues to the speaker that prove you are listening. Unfortunately, that means you need to put your cell phone back in your pocket. I would also suggest turning away from the laptop, and please, stop typing. (Ok, that's a pet peeve I have.) Look the speaker in the eye, and nod when you agree with the speaker. It's at that stage that I suggest you pay attention to your thoughts. This is the point most of us start to prepare a response. Give them the courtesy of hearing them. You may need to take a deep breath—another super power—to do this. It allows your rational mind to relax and allows you to hear.

Time:

Allot time to listen. This may be difficult at first, and I'm sure it will happen "on the fly" many times. Time is a gift we bestow on those we respect. By listening intently, you show the speaker that you respect them. With time comes the admonition to avoid interrupting the speaker. The only interruption you need is the one you give your brain to stop it from formulating that response. Interrupting the speaker only limits your ability to fully understand the message the speaker is delivering. It also introduces a chaotic energy into the discussion that also can inhibit real conversation. Just watch a panel of news analysts on one of the networks. They start interrupting each other and soon it becomes a loud shouting match and no one gets their points heard.

Comprehension:

Taking time to be sure we understand what is being said is important. How often have you spent 20 minutes discussing an issue then when you go to respond a short while later, you realize that you missed valuable information? Again, please don't beat yourself up. It happens all the time. We have our own filters that may block us from fully understanding. We have our own experiences, our own expectations that influence what we hear. It becomes our own interpretation not what was said. This is where two skills come in. First, ask clarifying questions when appropriate. These can be: "Can you expand on that..." or "What did you mean when you said..." Second, summarize your understanding. Examples include something as simple as, "Let me get this right, what I'm hearing is...."

Active listening allows you to hear the information as it was intended and telegraphs respect for the speaker. Once you get the information needed and clarified it, then you can formulate an informed response. It's a choice, another super power I might add, to spend the time to actively listen. It may mean a few quiet moments between you and the speaker, but with practice, you'll integrate those moments seamlessly.

I'll leave you with a few tips to help you get stronger as an influential leader:

- Leaders listen with full attention. They are 100 percent in the moment.
- Leaders are practiced at asking questions to pull information from their teams. They empower their people to think through an issue and creatively solve problems simply by listening.
- Leaders set examples by embodying active listening and modeling full attention. Those who practice active listening see immediate benefits when those around them respond positively.
- Leaders take care of themselves, allowing quiet time to work through the "voices in their heads." They know the downside of information overload and distraction.

In this distracted, over-informed world, keying into our innate super powers – to breathe, to choose and to listen – we allow ourselves to not only be more effective but to become the influencers we are meant to be. Harnessing distraction. Empowering others. Choosing the right course of action. You are a powerful leader!

Jeanne Alford

Communications and Media Coach

An experienced speaker, trainer, writer, and PR expert, Jeanne Alford spent her career honing her expertise in communications. She has directed national and international public affairs and public relations programs for several brands including Dolby, Philips Electronics, and Visa. She has also worked with leaders at some of the most innovative start-ups in Silicon Valley. No matter what position she held, her focus remains on telling a compelling branding story.

Jeanne's communications and PR campaigns have changed media perceptions, garnered national and international awareness for issues, and helped to strongly position executives as industry leaders. As an advocate for employee communications and crisis communications, she led programs to ensure that a company's most important asset, its people, are kept informed. As a trainer, she has assisted many executives in refining and leveraging their media efforts to ensure their company story is told through the eyes of respected media writers and broadcasters.

Today, Jeanne works with individuals and small businesses to tell their most captivating stories in the media, with customers, and among their colleagues. As a communications and media coach, she strives to apply those skills so her clients can tell their best stories using the most effective platforms. Her focus is on developing communications strategies and coaching business leaders to elevate and refine their message.

Jeanne, a best-selling co-author and writer, published several business articles, white papers, and marketing campaigns. Her materials have appeared in daily newspapers, national business publications, and on several online sites. She most recently authored "3 Magic Questions to Instantly Improve Your Communications," which is available to download at BeClear101.com.

Email: jeanne@alfordcommunications.com
Phone: 415-971-3344
Websites: alfordcommunications.com, beclear101.com
Facebook: https://www.facebook.com/
BeClear101-1896566077223594/
LinkedIn: https://www.linkedin.com/in/jeannealford
Twitter: @jealford

BOLD PEOPLE DO BOLD THINGS
BY CASSANDRA GARABEDIAN

"Nothing Comes To A Sleeper But A Dream" - *Unknown author*

Throughout my career if there was one underlying skill I have always relied on, it was my way with people. My comfort level was the same with all people regardless of race, creed, gender, or faith. I never felt limited from engaging with others. In fact, it did just the opposite and opened the way for me to strike up an authentic conversation. I've been told people tend to gravitate towards me and that they feel at ease speaking freely to me. There would be times when I would be engaged in conversation with someone and within minutes they would have told me their whole life story including intimate details you would normally only tell a close friend or relative. I would attribute their comfort level with me to my personable and compassionate nature. Sometimes I would share in conversation first, engaging in "light," carefree conversation. It would be a free-flowing friendly conversation to break the ice, especially with those people who exhibit the "elevator stare."

As with learning, different people communicate and perceive in different ways. Occasionally I have had to push aside my material possessions, because they were a distraction for the person with whom I was engaged in conversation. I did this so that I would have their undivided attention in order to enlighten them by showing them **material objects are just that—objects! They don't make a person, it's what's within that counts. Judge a person by their character.**

In life and in business, whether you are a model or a homemaker, an employee or the Founder and CEO of a business there will come a time when a situation arises that will test your character. Effective communication techniques will be imperative to build your brand, grow your business, strengthen relationships, and achieve your goals. In the following example, the Founder and CEO found her leadership style was challenged with the ultimate test. How well would she work under pressure?

There was a problem with programming a major piece of equipment used in the processing of a project. All work hinged on this part of the project and her company would not be able to keep its commitment to one of its most profitable clients if this project wasn't completed on time. The deadline was the next day, what would she do? By remaining calm and centered throughout the challenge, she did what any good leader would do—she led by example. She adopted an alternative process and procedure and began strategically planning, organizing, and analyzing the logistics and assigning her highly trained employees' ownership of this high priority project. To keep her commitment, she approved all the overtime to get the project completed and turned around on time. The deadline was met leaving her client thrilled once again with their work. Her character and creditability remained intact and no one outside of those working on the project knew what went on behind the scenes to get the job done. As with all challenges, there were lessons to be learned, such as having a backup supplier already in place.

Several days after the project was completed and the information was still fresh in their minds, the Founder and CEO called forth a team meeting to debrief the project. The team assigned to the project put together their list of ideas for the CEO. She learned from reading their list that they looked up to her because she led by example, that they felt that she's more than their employer, she's their trusted advisor. Her loyalty to them inspired their loyalty in return. They feel they have her support from the company culture in which she has built. The invaluable training, mentoring, special assignments, and outside events bring added value to what she offers her employees. But most of all it's her regular communication. She also learned her employees and the relationships she built with other businesses (B2B) were foremost the best! She couldn't have been as successful without the support from so many hands from afar, working just as hard and diligently as she and her employees. I was the CEO in this example. It takes a village. You can't see your vision through all by yourself and you will need the support of others.

It is my calling to bear witness to the purposeful life that was meant for me and to live to the best of my ability a life of sincerity, loyalty, and calmness. How I (and you) engage with others is a reflection of what is going on within me (you). Projecting a sense of trustworthiness, honesty, credibility, and positivity are characteristics that have served me well on my journey to be an entrepreneur. I believe people are an organization's greatest asset. I've been fortunate to have worked for some wonderful organizations throughout my career. They allowed me to develop, grow, stretch, explore new horizons and excel. I will always be grateful for all my experiences and the relationships that I have formed along the way. **In all that I do, it is my greatest desire to always be open and receptive, to never stop learning and to always be respectful of others.**

My first management position was for a retail store, as store manager. Although I didn't have prior work experience in the traditional sense, I was able to effectively lead my team members and manage the store by having the support of my team and my district manager, and winning several district and regional contests for our store. With strong communication skills working for me, my team and I achieved our monthly goals and team members projects. **I learned the importance of strategic planning for any organization in order to be successful.** I discovered the necessity of having great organizational skills and being people-oriented as important keys to success. These skills not only give you a competitive edge, but you will never train in vain.

Imagine people flocking to interview with you/your company because they have heard about your training program. Your company is known for giving workers their first shot, increasing their value through education, training, and people/customer experience. You treat your employees/customers with respect because you are people-oriented. You can create this culture within your organization. In return employers adopt the philosophy of Leigh Buchanan, "The way to win business is to mold your workers to fit your culture.."

It takes tenacity to be an entrepreneur. I recently attended an event where the guest speakers for the evening told inspiring tales of tenacity, entrepreneurs who refuse to give up. Those stories told on stage described how creative and resourceful entrepreneurs can be when their businesses are failing and they need to turn things around. **It takes courage, drive, and the will to take the risk to go against traditional methods. Being creative and thinking outside of the box has proven to be quite lucrative for some business models.**

Set goals that are achievable. If you're looking to achieve something great, and you want to stretch yourself and motivate and stretch your team to achieve their greatest potential, then set challenging goals along the way so that they can see what they are capable of. Rejection or missed goals are disappointing, and sometimes they can leave you broken, especially if you're an entrepreneur who is responsible for carrying the entire load of the company, you need to pay the bills, and make payroll. **Quitting isn't an option** when you have a family and you stand to lose your home and other assets. The only thing to do is to keep trying. There's an old saying, "When the going gets tough, the tough gets going." **You pick yourself up, no matter how hard, and get back out there.**

Depending on how you tend to view challenges—are they equivalent to "the glass being half full or half empty?"—will determine how view when you have failures. You shouldn't beat yourself up, instead celebrate them and learn from your mistakes, there are lessons to be had. As entrepreneur Leigh Buchanan said, "I wish I had bad days, because that means I am fighting and going forward. If you don't fall, that means you're not challenging yourself."

When it comes together it shows you have what it took all long, it just needed time to mature. But your work isn't over, you must sustain your position in a market that is forever changing, you must grow and thrive.

The market today is global and more dynamic than ever. As an entrepreneur you must keep your pulse on what it is that is driving your industry.

Thinking outside of the box for the most part is what enabled the company in this example's success. The CEO believes if you're an expert in something, you may be trained to think in a certain way and not necessarily to ask big questions, but when you're new or young, you may be more inclined to ask, "Why do people do things in this way? Why has this been the case for so long?" Whether you are for or against such practices, I think we can all agree it allows everyone the power to tackle complex problems in new ways.

Quoted in the chapter Leigh Buchanan. You'll Never Train in Vain: The way to win business is to mold your workers to fit your culture.

Business Leadership Success Tips:

1. Be open and respectful.
2. Never stop learning.
3. Develop a strategic plan to follow.
4. Be willing to be tenacious and courageous.
5. Set challenging goals.
6. Quitting isn't an option. Failure is a learning opportunity.
7. **Keep going** to bring yourself, your company, and your vision forward.

Cassandra Garabedian

Cassandra Garabedian is a co-author, style consultant, and the Founder and CEO of Making Statements N Style. Cassandra's flair for style is anything but conventional; she has an amazing talent for capturing the true essence and lifestyle of a woman. Cassandra's goal is to create a look that is comfortable, appropriate for the occasion, and is polished, "put-together," a look that has an effortless appeal to it.

Cassandra's creativity, prior work experience, education, and travel experience have given way for professionals, entrepreneurs, and business women alike to experience what it feels like to dress with purpose, for success, and still look stylish. Cassandra coined the phrase, "Fashion With A Purpose."

Cassandra has built "signature looks" that resonate "beauty"—the kind of beauty that comes from within—confidence, character, respect, friendships as well as other characteristics that are awaiting to step forward and shine.

A former runway model, she has walked the catwalk in some of San Francisco's and other West Coast cities' most prominent fashion shows, to the catwalks of the fashion houses of Milan, Italy. She has studied fashion design in San Francisco, she held an apprentice position at a small design company, and she was mentored by a former head seamstress at Levi Strauss, Co., SF. An entrepreneur in her own right, Cassandra is now inspiring others to follow their passions in life, to never let go of their passion to go after them, to not let anything stand in their way, and to try not to have any regrets in life when it comes to their career. The thing that you live for, of one day attaining it, being successful at it, however success is supposed to look to you, that's what's counts if you're not hurting anyone. Do you.

Cassandra received a BS degree in Business Management double majoring in Marketing at the University of San Francisco. Thirteen years of corporate work experience in banking and merchant services, payment fraud & cryption as a relationship manager and credit card professional.

Email: cgarabedian@gmail.com
Phone: (510) 755-5903
Website: www.makingstatementsnstyle.com
Making Statements 'N Style Facebook Address:
https://www.facebook.cypom/Making-Statements-N-Style-205396
4941541986/
Facebook: https://www.facebook.com/cassandraf.garabedian.9
Twitter: https://twitter.com/cgarabed53

THE CURIOUS LEADER
BY BONNIE BONADEO

I always wondered where the expression "curiosity killed the cat" came from. We all know that cats are notorious for taking risks and supposedly having nine lives. So, I did some research and what I found was: "Inquisitiveness can lead one into dangerous situations." Along with that, the expression, *curiosity killed the cat*, had been changed over the years and as far back as 1598 and it went like this: curiosity replaced the word care, *care killed the cat*, meaning the coiner of the expression meant worry/sorry rather than the more usual contemporary "look after or provide for" meaning we know today. *Care* (worry/sorrow) *killed the cat* would mean that care (caring too much) would wear them all out. Inquisitiveness, worry, sorrow, caring and being placed in dangerous situations may be why most mediocre leaders don't understand or take to heart the power of curiosity in their leadership role.

Here is what I know for sure – as humans, we have a very strong desire to be right, judge, protect ourselves, our ego, our position, and our status. Being curious or even caring too much has a level of vulnerability that may make it difficult for even the best leaders to feel powerful or be respected in their position.

Let's dive into curiosity some more. I get the very old adage now on *care killed the cat*. As leaders, we tend to worry and feel sorrow when the pressure is on for us to direct, produce, and deliver on company commitments. We may think that engaging in care and careful manner is too soft, we may even believe that being overtly curious when leading others is manipulative and or hitting a grey area in our personal/business communication style. But I want you to think about this: if I, as a leader, don't know the answer to the situation as to why a team member is having problems, such as behavior issues or performance issues, my only opportunity is to start by asking questions coming from a place of curiosity (vs. going right into policy, write-ups or sending them off to HR).

In our roles as high-level leaders, more than 87% of the time, things go as they should. However, there is always the inevitable 13% when a situation arises that we must take on our true leadership role of being present, leading people, and managing systems. This is when we need to be *The Curious Leader*.

The biggest mistake I see many leaders of all levels make is not being present or curious and misunderstand the difference among leading, managing, and coaching.

The saying goes... lead people, manage systems and policies. **The Curious Leader understands people are their greatest asset and resource and allows for compassionate collaboration in communication with fair and in some cases flexible systems to be available.** Approaching leadership as a coach is a great way to avoid these top five mistakes I see leaders make.

Five Mistakes We Can Make When We Forget Curiosity:

1. We don't ask enough questions to get enough information
2. We are asking the wrong questions or leading questions
3. We over direct in leading vs. leading by engagement
4. We manage by policy and not humanness
5. We assume everyone understands their role and has the same strengths

Mistake #1: We don't ask enough questions to get enough information

Let me begin by clarifying a leadership metric when we are faced with having to have a difficult conversation or meeting with another (this qualifies in any situation, not just a business role; family and relationships apply here as well). As a curious leader, we must first determine and be curious enough to define the problem and lead the outcome in one of these two ways:

Is it a:

1. Behavior Issue (being late, leaving early, being disruptive, being gossipy, or creating animosity in the work culture) or is it a
2. Performance Issue (not producing the results, below the measurable expectations, unable to complete the work or project of high quality and in a timely manner).

As a leader, I must first ask myself the critical and curious questions:

- Do I know for a fact that this person is having performance issues? If you can answer yes because you have documented metrics, then you can move on to the next question.
- Do I know for a fact that this person is having behavioral issues? This one is much harder to diagnose and to secure the facts as you may have to witness this first for it to be fact.

The Curious Leader Tip: Look at your expectations of self and communication style. What are you projecting onto your team that may be creating confusion or unclear expectations? Are you being too direct, passive, or avoiding communicating at all? Which fear response do you have that may be creating a poor work culture or undesirable outcomes? Do you have a tendency toward fight, flight, or freeze?

Mistake #2: We are asking the wrong questions or leading questions

Is there such a thing as a wrong question? Yes, there is, if it disguised as a statement or is directed with a passive-aggressive approach. A statement is defined as a question that ends in a question mark, but you already know the answer to the question. Here is an example: Did you finish the project analysis that I requested to be done yesterday?

There are two parts to this statement:

1. You know the answer, and you are thinking you are being inquisitive by asking a question vs. just asking where the report is and what may be the reason it is not complete yet.
2. Adding the second part to the statement confirms you know the answer as you would have the report otherwise and you would not have asked the question.

Asking a question like this does two things to the person you are asking:

- It triggers the defense mechanism in their brain to protect themselves and potentially give them time to defend and think of an excuse (no leader or manager has time for this).
- Because you already know the answer, it creates a form of mistrust in the mind of the other person and mistrust triggers our fear responses of fight, flight, or freeze. This will cause them to challenge you or avoid you at all costs (again no leader has time for this, and this is not creating a strong culture in the organization).

The Curious Leader Tip: There are five styles of questions to support great dialogues and creative solutions:

1. **Yes/no** (the answer is either/or and does not engage but may be necessary to ask during a dialogue – this triggers defense system most of the time).
2. **Closed-end** (expecting an answer without story or excuses, just the facts, but again may trigger defense system).
3. **Open-end** (engages open dialogue and the thinking part of the brain).
4. **Multiple Choice** (requests them to choose one over the other and engages commitment as they have chosen vs. being told again engages the thinking part of the brain).
5. **Open Information** (provide a story or scenario with the questions being added to the backend – this supports caring, compassion, and empathy and engages both the analytical and emotional part of the brain).

Mistake #3: We over direct in leading vs. leading by engagement:

Overdirecting could translate to micromanaging and most employees will tell you that a micromanager is the worst. This translates to mistrust, and with the dynamics of so many generations in the workforce today, most employees are looking to be a greater contribution to the big picture and how their job role relates to that. Just like overdirecting as a leader, asking leading questions puts people on the defense as if they have done something wrong, Leading questions are also a form of a statement; they are designed to make you think but can feel personal and targeted; when leading people, they can feel accusatory and belittling.

The Curious Leader Tip: Asking a question vs. telling another what you want from them is always going to have a more favorable outcome and engaged commitment. Here's an example. Based on what I have requested, are you comfortable moving forward with this project? Wait for a reply, acknowledge and ask another open-information question. For example, you can ask: "You know, we are looking to launch this in the spring, so we want to make sure we have tested everything by the end of the month. What concerns do you have with these timelines?" Wait for a reply, acknowledge and ask a final question, for example a multiple choice question: "I would like to check in with you as we progress. What is acceptable for you on these check-ins, twice a week or once a week?" As you can see, they are getting to participate in the conversation with you and the engagement, and commitment goes up!

Mistake #4: We manage by policy and not humanness

Managing by policy is sometimes a rookie mistake we make as a new leader, but I see this mistake happen more often than it should with even the most seasoned of leaders. When you manage too much by policy you remove the human side of the leader role which eliminates empathy and compassion. Yes, we all should have clear systems and policies in place to support growth in the company and among personnel, but great leaders put humanness first and look for the unknown reason why the existing circumstance is present. Curious leaders also understand stuff happens and it can be easily resolved with open communication vs. the "you know our policy..." approach (which triggers the defense system). I am a firm believer that if you are dealing with a repeat offender of issues that you should consider looking at your leadership skills as a first step and seeing where you can improve awareness, communication, and listening skills.

The Curious Leader Tip: The minute we manage by policy we have triggered the fear response system, which is solely designed to protect our ego self. It is counter-intuitive to be an effective leader and uncover what may be behind the performance or behavior issue to progress in changing that behavior. The #1 reason stated as to why people leave their jobs is management and lack of communication by management. Always err on the side of communicating. Download my free template of The A.A.A.S.K. Method that will support you with a formula for effective communication. https://www.bonniebonadeo.com/the-curious-leader

Mistake #5: We assume everyone understands their role and has the same strengths

The Curious Leaders understand not only their own strengths but also their weaknesses. They realize that building a strong culture and team is about blended strengths and weaknesses. More important than that is building a team with open communication on what I call a Personal Brand Strategy, which is understanding what makes each person unique as a contributor. With blended workforces and project management styles, the Personal Brand Strategy allows for the cross-contribution of personal strengths to be recognized and developed. We all know that certain labels and titles prevent effective and open communication within organizations.

The Curious Leader Tip: Reprimand in private and recognize in public. This is the easiest way for leaders to build community – acknowledge the greatness each team member is contributing and openly express that. This triggers positive enforcement of others and develops the atmosphere of team members engaging with each other vs. always having to go to the leader for questions.

My love for leadership is based on my personal brand and strategy as a *Connector*. Like many of us, I have learned the hard way on my leadership style and communication skills. I'm very aware of my driven and results focused approach to make progress and I do believe leaders are both born and made to be great. I am the perfect example of that and when I up leveled my coaching skills to be more inquisitive and curious my leadership became recognized and rewarded.

Developing your curiosity skills will certainly improve your leadership skills along with building a great culture of support and trust in the workplace. Of course, all these skills can be used outside of work and in our personal lives as well. They are designed to strengthen relationships and eliminate the stress that leaders endure, because they always feel like they need to know or have all the answers.

The Curious Leader knows they don't have to have all the answers, but they do need to ask more questions. When we let our truth, authentic style, along with our humanness come forth, the problems seem to more easily resolve themselves. The Curious Leader supports their people being the best version of who they are and the amazing contribution they can bring to the team, company, and community. Being a curious leader will provide you with the satisfaction of a job well done.

Curiosity may have killed the cat, but satisfaction and deep care brought it back.

Bonnie Bonadeo

Bonnie Bonadeo – Speaker-Coach-Author-Audio Influencer, Bonnie is known as The Connection Coach plus Founder of The Beauty Agent Network Speaker –Educator Resource, The Education Agents, and, BonnieBonadeo.com—Coach & Speaker, and Syndicated Host and Audio Influencer and International Best-Selling Author.

Bonnie focuses on the people part of leadership, personal branding, and public speaking. By eliminating "overused and overrated techniques" and layers of "how to's" she coaches others to uncover and discover their greatness and what is takes to elicit greatness in others. She has trained and coached hundreds of entrepreneurs and C-Suite Leaders to be better speakers and build a strong personal and company brand.

A beauty and wellness industry professional with over 25 years of experience, she has mastered many levels and achievements. As a 2013 Enterprising Women and 2016 Cover of Salon Today Coaches Guide, she is a Certified Emotional Intelligent Speaker, Executive Business Coach, 4x International Best-selling Author of "Success in Beauty" and "Empowering You and Transforming Lives," The Power of 50, plus a syndicated Radio

Host, podcaster, and audio influencer to over 50,000 listeners monthly on BEaUty Inside and Out Show.

Bonnie speaks authentically on her struggles and successes as a person, leader, speaker, and entrepreneur to foster growth and awareness in others. She is the essence of being the beauty agent and of her brand which is all about Connecting You to You!

Bonnie@BonnieBonadeo.com
623-810-9663 (cell) 877-319-2403 (Biz)
www.BonnieBonadeo.com
https://www.facebook.com/BonnieBonadeoCoach/
https://www.facebook.com/Beautyinsideandoutshow/
https://www.facebook.com/TheBeautyAgentNetwork/
https://www.linkedin.com/in/bonniebonadeo/
https://twitter.com/bonniebonadeo1
https://www.youtube.com/channel/
UCKEJunJ5YUs0Wao-rtZoE8g?view_as=subscriber
https://www.instagram.com/bonniebonadeo/

SIX HEART-CENTERED ACTIONS OF A PASSION POWERED L.E.A.D.E.R™!
BY ANITA TORRES

"If your actions inspire others to dream more, learn more, do more, and become more, you are a leader." - John Quincy Adams

My Early Experience

WHACK! WHACK! WHACK! These were the sounds that resonated throughout the classroom as Sister Bernadette cracked the ruler down upon my nine-year-old hands—all for not knowing the answer to six plus four. I'll never forget how mortified, embarrassed, angry, and utterly confused I felt. With tears pouring out of my little-girl eyes, I made my way, as ordered, back to my seat; the same seat I had wished would swallow me up just minutes earlier to avoid being called upon. I remember thinking, "A teacher is supposed to help students learn and to discover the answer." This experience profoundly impacted my early views of authority and leadership. I decided then that Sister Bernadette was not a great leader or teacher. This was a life-changing, life-defining experience that I recall now more than ever, as I reflect on my own leadership journey and what it means to be an inspiring leader–in education, in a business, as part of an organization, a team, a charity, a cause, or a classroom—and what the specific actions are that make a great leader—A Passion Powered L.E.A.D.E.R™.

"Passion is energy. Feel the power that comes from focusing on what excites you." Oprah Winfrey

Leading with Passion

Thankfully, through the years, I have been blessed with many great teachers, mentors, and bosses who have taught me what WORKS and what DOES NOT WORK as a leader. What has made the biggest difference in my experience of the leaders in my life is PASSION. People and clients often ask me, "What's passion got to do with leading?" I say EVERYTHING! Passion is not just for the bedroom; it works in the boardroom too! Passion is an intense emotion, a compelling feeling, an overwhelming desire, or an all-consuming enthusiasm for something or someone. Passion is contagious, it shakes things up, wakes up your workforce, and brings life and vitality to an organization's mission, vision, and core values!

Have you ever felt unmotivated at work or have known someone on your team that is disengaged or who is a bit checked out? I think we've all been there or have known someone who has been or is currently disengaged. I'm not surprised one bit. Gallup's (https://news.gallup.com/poll/241649/employee-engagement-rise.aspx) research indicates, as of June 2018, that only 34% of the American workforce is actively engaged, meaning they are emotionally connected to their work within the workplace; 53% are not engaged, meaning they are getting by doing minimal work, and 13% are actively disengaged (they are miserable in their work situations). In fact, managers are the reason for 70% of the variance in employee engagement. Disengaged managers create disengaged employees.

The good news is that LEADERS hold the golden key to improve these engagement numbers through their interactions, recognitions, and coaching opportunities with each team member to improve performance and leverage individual strengths. My passion (and purpose) in life and business is in guiding leaders and managers to increase the employee engagement numbers in their organizations. When you take away the four walls of an organization and all the data analytics and tools to run the business, what is left are the people that matter most and make it all happen. **Passionate leaders create actively engaged and passionate employees.**

Afterall, where do we spend most of our days? We are at work, contributing to bosses, teams, and customers. Employees want to make a difference one person at a time or in the world and passionate leaders can help them do just that.

We are all leaders, everyday leaders, and one does not need a formal title to demonstrate leadership qualities and take powerful actions. Take a moment for yourself now and reflect on the attributes and actions of your best leader or role model in your life–someone whom you aspire to be like or has taught you many great lessons. What words would you use to describe him or her? What specific actions did he or she take? How did he or she make you feel? I can imagine you may have said something similar to how my own mentors have inspired me. In fact, Maya Angelou's famous saying sums up, most eloquently, what I say about leaders and why research indicates employees leave the manager more than the job:

"I've learned people will forget what you said, people will forget what you did, but people will never forget how you made them feel."

Take a moment to re-read the quote and replace the word "people" with "employees" and you will feel Angelou's powerful message is most appropriate in the workplace. Now, I'm not suggesting that leaders must be soft, mushy, or lovey-dovey all the time to be best leaders. The leaders that stand out most are those who are powered by passion and produce amazing results with their teams!

Actions of a Passion Powered L.E.A.D.E.R™

As we explore the actions of a Passion Powered Leader™, see if your inspirational leader or role model is described here. If you aspire to be a leader of a project, a team, or a business, consider taking on these actions to build an actively engaged workforce. If you are a leader today, take a personal inventory to see where your leadership is strong and where you might want to improve. Along the way, I will share with you examples of the leaders that inspired me.

Loves Serving Others

Leading from the heart begins with having a genuine love for serving others. This lesson was deeply ingrained in me by the late Delia Maria

Fernandez, my mom. Mom was the epitome of servant leadership. She was a full-time mom, a community volunteer, a facilitator of Bible study groups, a Eucharistic minister, and the lead actress playing the role of the *Virgin Mary* in the church's annual *Passion of the Christ* plays. In small and big ways, she loved all the people whose lives she touched. Love was the center of all her intentions, actions, and decisions. In my professional career, I've experienced leaders who were promoted for their technical knowledge and expertise but who were lacking in their interpersonal and emotional intelligence skills—skills that should have been founded upon an honest fondness for the people they led. If this is an area you'd like to learn and improve on, and it can be done, then commit to first loving yourself enough to invest in your own personal and professional development to reach positive milestones as a servant leader. Expand your emotional intelligence skills to enhance your self-awareness and to understand your emotions, and the emotions of others, which leads to making better decisions and developing better relationships.

Engages Authentically

I have had the honor to be coached and mentored by the late Judith E. Glaser, author of *Conversational Intelligence: How Leaders Build Trust and Get Extraordinary Results*. In her 30+ years of research, she discovered that "To get to the next level of greatness depends on the quality of our culture, which depends on the quality of our relationships, which depends on the quality of our conversations. Everything happens through conversation." You see, conversations have a way of shutting people down or opening people up. Our brains are wired to generate either high cortisol (the stress hormone) or oxytocin (the happy or love hormone) during conversations. Leaders who succeed in raising the passion levels in the workplace engage authentically by listening to connect, not judge or reject. They ask powerful questions for which they have no answers and they prime the conversation to establish trust. These are just a few of the vital interpersonal skills that cannot be over emphasized as core leadership competencies.

Appreciates Sincerely

Dr. Rita Smith was the best leader **with whom, not for whom** I've worked in the mid-1990s. These highlighted words make the difference in how she worked with and appreciated others. Dr. Rita Smith never left great work or good effort go unnoticed. I have kept every email or handwritten card I received from her and others on our team. We all got to know her as a genuine person and as an extraordinary leader. She made time to get to know each team member, sincerely shared herself with us and was always willing to roll up her sleeves and pitch in when she could. Dr. Rita Smith was a caring, courageous leader who was also firm but fair and who spoke with candor when needed. She emulated the words of Teddy Roosevelt, "Nobody cares how much you know until they know how you care." How often are you appreciating sincerely? Don't underestimate the power of these simple words and phrases: "please," "thank you," and "I appreciate you for..."

Demonstrates Core Values

How many times have you seen and read the "mission and vision" plaques on the lobby walls of an organization? Leaders who bring life and vitality to the company's mission and vision are those who demonstrate the vision and values through their actions and behaviors. Leading by example is top of mind. If you value starting meetings on time, then you, the leader, must always be the first to live that value. Judith E. Glaser, Dr. Rita Smith, and Mom were amazing leaders who lived, breathed, and consistently modeled their core values. Core values are at the center of everything a business does, and they help build a strong foundation. Strong core values are sustainable, constant, motivating, personal, and applicable. Whether you are an aspiring leader, a start-up business owner, or have a thriving business, get clear about your passions and values, review your business processes, and check each area against your core values. Develop new processes that better align with core values, if necessary. Communicate core values across the organization and display them prominently where every employee, from top to bottom, can see them.

Embraces Team Spirit

The best way to embrace team spirit is through celebration. One of my favorite memories when working with Dr. Rita Smith is when our entire team paraded through the company, celebrating a successful completion of a project. We would apply marketing techniques to launch and promote our team projects. We created brochures, posters, and distributed promotional items to employees. We even carried a boom box with Kool & The Gang's "Celebrate" song while we paraded. It was so much fun to celebrate success. We didn't parade around for every project. Sometimes we would all meet in a conference room, share a celebratory cake, write personal notes of acknowledgement and read them aloud to each team member. Not only did Dr. Rita Smith prepare executive summary reports of project results for senior leadership, she also made sure each of us was recognized for our part in the team project. Don't wait for big projects to come to full completion. Celebrate individual and team successes along the way. Practice management by walking around to catch people doing things right and give acknowledgment for them. Be sure to tailor the acknowledgement based on the preferences of each team member.

Reinforces Goals & Expectations

The most critical step in leadership is setting clear business goals and expectations for achieving them. However, just setting them in the beginning of the year is not enough. Reinforcing goals and expectations throughout the year keeps employees on track, highly engaged, and productive. Leaders who provide coaching and support along the way to achieving goals create a culture that emphasizes *we're on this path together*. For example, Dr. Rita Smith guided, helped, and coached us to improve performance based on the goals and expectations she set for the team and the organization. She taught us how to be resourceful, to think critically, and to be problem-solvers. How? By letting the team know she was available to help in any way on the condition that we present our case having thought through at least two to three possible solutions to address the issue or problem. This was a very powerful strategy that not only helped her reinforce goals but also empowered us to develop our own leadership skills.

Results of a Passion Powered L.E.A.D.E.R™

I am grateful to my leaders, and yes, even to Sister Bernadette, for all these lessons learned that I was fortunate to apply in my own role as a manager/leader. Today, I am on a professional mission to inspire leaders to communicate simply, to engage teams powerfully, to thrive in their businesses, and to be leaders worth following. Through executive leadership coaching, team development training, and/or organizational consulting, my clients have developed trusting relationships, experienced increased productivity, higher retention, and improved self-awareness—to name a few results. It takes COMMITMENT for a leader in any business to create a company culture that is infused with passion, fun, and authenticity, productivity, accountability, and results. It takes COURAGE for a leader to look within and do some homework which I lovingly refer to as "OM work." This self-reflection "OM work" is intended for leaders to get clear with personal passions, to align mission with core values and core behaviors, to learn and apply new skills, and to work with a passionate, results-driven executive leadership coach. I had the pleasure of working with a business owner of a health and wellness center who leads a team of five in the practice. She was experiencing high turnover, team conflict, and lost productivity. What she desired most was to create a "Dream Team" that produces amazing results and to improve communication with her team. What her team needed most was clear direction and purpose, specific goals and expectations, learning resources and tools to support them to succeed. During our coaching engagement and through structured interviews and assessments, we uncovered that the leader could improve her listening and questioning skills as well as developing more structured processes and policies. The leader agreed to engage in one-on-one coaching sessions to gain clarity on her core passions and values, to focus on communication, and to improve processes. We also conducted team workshops and brainstorming sessions to involve the staff in creating and supporting the "Dream Team" goals, expectations, and accountabilities. This process involves training and coaching employees who are ready and willing to contribute to the overall success of the practice. Today, the "Dream Team" is in place and primed for great success. The leader is listening and connecting more with the each staff member. Training materials and operational documentation are clearly written leaving no room for misinterpretation.

You can achieve great results too! After all, how you give something is equally as important as what that something is. In retrospect had I known then what I know now, I would tell my nine-year-old, and possibly Sister Bernadette, it's not enough to be in a position of leadership. What matters most is how you choose to lead. Practice the actions of a Passion Powered L.E.A.D.E.R today, not someday!

Here is a quick summary of mindsets and actions you can take today to be a Passion Powered L.E.A.D.E.R™ :

1. **L**ove Serving Others
2. **E**ngage Authentically
3. **A**ppreciate Sincerely
4. **D**emonstrate Core Values
5. **E**mbrace Team Spirit
6. **R**einforce Goals & Expectations

Anita Torres

Meet Anita, the Passionista, Torres

Passionate leaders, engaged employees, better conversations produces powerful results. That's what Anita lives for. Facilitating performance improvement within teams, individuals, and organizations. That's where her passion begins. Anita Torres brings her "New York" and "Miami" energy to everything she does. She is a highly motivated and passionate Certified Executive Leadership Coach and Consultant. Her purpose and mission are to inspire leaders to communicate simply, to engage teams powerfully, to thrive in business and life, and BE leaders worth following through coaching and consulting. With 20+ years in the talent development space, elite certifications, and a Master's degree in Instructional Systems, Anita gets to the heart of the individual, team, and/or organizational performance gaps with solutions that best address goals and needs. She takes pride in designing and delivering quality, effective, and efficient professional development programs that cultivate top performance at work, at home, and in life. Her signature program includes critical elements of her Passion Powered Formula for Leadership Success™: Passionate Leaders + Powerful Communication + Productive Teams = Profitable Results.

Anita's workshops and speaking engagements are highly interactive, filled with passion, energy, and lots of key learning takeaways to apply immediately at work and in life. Don't be surprised to see the audience up and out of their chairs networking, laughing, dancing, and engaging in experiential activities that touch the mind, heart, and soul. Anita customizes programs and presentations to fit all learning needs, audiences, and adds some fun to the experience. Anita has presented for the Central Florida Chapter of Association for Talent Development, National Customer Service Association Summit and Conference, Michigan Society of Association Executives, East Lake County Chamber of Commerce, Lake-Sumter State College, Keiser University, Columbia University, the Reinvention Convention and Retreat, and the YouFirst Women's Conference and Retreat.

Email: Anita@PassionPoweredLeadership.com
Cell: 352-455-4869
www.PassionPoweredLeadership.com
https://www.facebook.com/PassionPoweredLeadership
linkedin.com/in/passionpoweredleadership
twitter.com/BeAPassionista
YouTube Channel: https://www.youtube.com/channel/
UCCRP_PNTSesvyAc049sTSSw/featured?view_as=public

LEADING IN THE SPOTLIGHT: DO YOU LISTEN?
BY ROSEMARIE BARNES

Have you ever felt that although you are talking, no one is listening?

If you are a business, that can be a terrible thing! Is your audience disinterested? Are they distracted? Are they uncomfortable? How can you engage them? Perhaps they are tired of hearing all about **you**. The essence of communication is speaking and listening and that can only happen if the spotlight is shared.

Relationships are the core of good businesses and good business practices and rely on give-and-take to create mutually beneficial processes and results. This is not news nor is it newsworthy, but it is **vital.**

If you want to be heard, you must first learn to listen. If you want to be seen, you must first learn to see, and what's more, you must learn to listen and see with neutrality, so you can observe what is really there. Especially as leaders, it is easy to see and hear what we **want** to see and hear because we color it from our own point of view. We send information through our own filters, not those of others, and then wonder why we don't really "get" the point others are trying to make.

The most common complaint from young people is, "No one listens to me!" We've probably all heard a parent's exasperation when they talk about their children and say, "They just don't listen!" For the energetic and enthusiastic business up-and-comers, the most difficult hurdle is getting "heard" by the right ears, those ears being the ones that truly listen for potential. For possibility. From the other side of the fence, have you ever witnessed perplexed leaders puzzled at why they aren't getting the "buy-in" from their teams?

For the most part, the problem is that while the receiving ears are "hearing" what we are saying, they are interpreting that information through their own filters, which have served them well in the past. Convincing others to adopt a new point of view is as difficult as getting someone to change their value system and that is probably the most difficult thing we could every attempt. We cannot understand the complexities of that attempt until we have taken the opportunity to reconsider and possibly alter our own filters and values, and that is a massive undertaking.

That's the trick to it all; creating lasting relationships requires learning to see and hear not from our own position and biases, but from theirs.

Not Simple. Not Easy.

It takes a very self-aware person to have confidence enough to even momentarily put aside their own ideas and opinions, to honestly and openly listen, and whole-heartedly try to understand the other party's needs and strengths.

Listening, even active listening, is not enough. The old adage of "Walk a mile in their shoes" is the key to understanding, and understanding is essential for true communication. Anything less is only lip service which does more to undermine relationships than even condescension or aloofness. At least with those, both parties are clear about where they stand.

The word of the day is "solipsistic." It is derived from Sol (the sun, perceived in days long past as the center of the universe) and ipsis (a state of being), the resultant meaning being believing oneself to be the center of the universe with all other heavenly bodies orbiting around only them.

Babies are born in a completely self-centered or solipsistic state. When they are tired, hungry, wet, bored, and so on, they don't care what their caregiver is doing, whether the caregiver is exhausted, or anything else about the caregiver. Babies want what they want, and they want it now! They have no language skills so there is no way to tell them they are being unreasonable or that if they would only wait five minutes their dilemma will be solved.

Babies don't share the spotlight with anyone! A baby must be taught that they are not the only being in existence and that others have needs, too. Some of us take longer to learn that lesson than others, and some learn it better than others; is there anyone that doesn't know individuals that, even as adults, continue to live in their solipsistic bubbles? Since most adults have language skills, they may either be choosing not to use them or use them well, OR they may simply not care enough to be bothered to try to understand others' situations.

Now, there is a great deal of validity and truth that if we don't see to our own needs first, we are not as well equipped to assist others; the case of the oxygen masks in airplanes is a case in point, but relationships are not grounded in emergency procedures. Relationships depend on reciprocity and caring, and **then** on clear communication.

Let's talk for a moment about the Law of Reciprocity.

The Law of Reciprocity says that when someone receives a gift they perceive to be valuable, they immediately feel an urge to "return the favor." If someone does something nice for you, you consciously or subconsciously look for ways to do something nice in return. It works in reverse as well: if you do something nice for someone, you expect them to favor you in kind, at some point, and in some way. **If a leader makes an effort to make an individual feel special and valued, for example, it is usually repaid with loyalty and an increased desire to prove the leader was right to hold that positive opinion.**

Conversely, if an individual diligently applies his or herself to completing an assignment or task in record time and with extraordinary quality and does **not** receive a commendation from the leader, he or she may well feel affronted and resentful at the lack of what they feel to be rightfully owed attention. The Law of Reciprocity was not fulfilled, and the debt not paid.

Project work is a perfect example. If two individuals are assigned a joint project, and each believe they have contributed approximately equally, they expect equal compensation. When kudos are handed out for a job well done, both individuals reasonably expect equal time in the spotlight. If that doesn't happen, if one of the individuals takes sole credit or minimizes the contributions of the other, it will be considered a breach of trust, of respect, and hard feelings will **always** be the result.

A single episode may be forgiven or overlooked, but a repeat performance of "hogging the spotlight" will demand a re-evaluation of the relationship, where apologies may help to heal the wound, or if the breach of trust has been severe, the relationship may come to a harsh full stop. It is possible to stack the favor bank if the relationship is firmly established, but at some point, the stack will topple, and the relationship will suffer.

Today we have an additional complication with the Law of Reciprocity.

The Baby Boomers and Generation X (individuals born post war to about 1980) are **bound** by this Law and it governs much of their personal and professional behavior. Generation Y (Millennials:1980-2000) and Z (Edgers: post 2000) do not live by this rule, and for the most past, are not even aware of its existence. Because these younger generations do not experience the urge to reciprocate, or at least not at the same levels of the previous generations, favor and kindness debts awarded to Gen Y or Z are gratefully accepted and then not given a second thought by the recipients.

In great numbers, Baby Boomers and Generation X live, eat, and breathe reciprocity, and when no repayment arrives, they tend to experience a flood of negativity toward the recipient of their gift or favor, and the seeds of resentment and distrust are planted.

On the other side of the equation, Gen Y and Z are not as uniformly bound by the need to reciprocate, or that there is any obligation attached to kindness, favors, or sharing credit. When **they** provide those services to others, including the older generations, they expect nothing in return except a sincere thank you. They are more likely to accept the feel-good emotions that accompany their generosity to be payment enough. It is rare to find Gen Y and Z individuals doing something nice for someone because they want to stock up their favor bank. They tend to perceive the whole system of "owing a favor back" to be inane and silly. It is simply not a value they accept.

They do, however, readily accept that teamwork is the fastest road to success, and they are accustomed to working in groups to achieve desired outcomes. This is very different from their predecessors who took great pride in being able to accomplish things purely on their own. For Baby

Boomers and Generation X, sharing the spotlight in business was much more difficult than it is for Millennials.

Very recently, I listened to *Outliers* by Malcolm Gladwell wherein he talks about the notion of being a self-made success. In the book he details the difficulties of the past within Korean airlines where airplane crashes and safety concerns actually had a number of countries disallowing them into their airspace. More accidents happened within that airline than any other in the world even though pilots went through rigorous training programs and the aircrafts were in excellent condition.

Turns out it was a communication problem caused by societal expectations. In Korea at the time (and even today) respect, especially for higher ranking officers, demanded that captain's orders be obeyed and not questioned. In the case of the airline, even if the captain was exhausted by too many hours in the cockpit, second officers and other crew did not question actions even if they thought them to be in error. Surely their superior knew better than they, else they would not be sitting in the left seat, and to have suggested an error in judgement would be construed as an insult of the highest order.

In North America, while the chain of command is equally required, co-pilots are expected to do more than simply obey, and when the lives of hundreds of passengers are in their care, pilots and crew are expected to work as a team to ensure the safety of all.

That means communicating clearly, effectively, and efficiently, especially in times of crisis.

Consider the more recent case of Captain Sully gliding his passenger jet to safely land in the Hudson River after both engines ceased to function. He was in the control seat and his commands needed to be heard, but it was a team effort to save the lives of 155 passengers and crew. Captain Sully did not take full credit for the landing, but instead, shared the spotlight with every single crew member on that flight even though he was in charge.

The result? He earned the respect of the crew, the airline, the media, and the world.

And why did he do it? Because no man is an island, especially on the Hudson River, and he is an excellent leader that genuinely cares about those he works with. Had he taken all the credit, he would have risked his relationships with all of them.

It's easy to share the spotlight when you value the contributions of the team. Most of us do, but perhaps we have not fully realized it or perhaps we haven't taken the time to express it.

Sharing the spotlight doesn't demean our contributions, or tamper with control over our teams or the situations. Sharing the spotlight simply means giving credit where credit is due and communicating appreciation or gratitude in a significant or meaningful way. It means developing and nurturing an Attitude of Gratitude for the contributions of others and then making an effort to share the sincere appreciation.

It doesn't matter whether you are a child or a grandparent, an up-and-comer, or a seasoned business leader, the core of communication is more about listening than talking. Even solipsistic babies learn to listen before they learn to speak. The secret sauce though is to listen by making a solid effort to "hear" from the other party's point of view.

After that, sharing the spotlight becomes reasonable, rational, and in the business world, the most profitable thing to do.

My name is Rosemarie Barnes. My company is Confident Stages. It exists to champion others to become comfortable and confident regardless of the stage they are in or the stage they are on. To that end, Confident Stages offers me as a keynote speaker on the topics of bridging the generation gaps in business, and navigating through personal, professional, and corporate reinvention and transformation, as well as the value of powerful public speaking skills.

I champion leaders to step into the spotlight confidently and effectively so that they can lead powerfully.

Here are some Leadership Tips to support you in the spotlight:

1. Listen
2. Gain Understanding
3. Show Appreciation
4. Share the Spotlight
5. SHINE!

I'd love to have a conversation with you and can be reached through my website www.confidentstages.com or via direct email rbarnes@confidentstages.com.

I can and will champion you and your teams to Speak to Engage, Speak to Succeed for your relationships, your business, and your life.

Rosemarie Barnes

Rosemarie Barnes is passionate about leadership and executive talent development.

Coming from an eclectic background involving theatre, music, and business, Rosemarie believes that especially in this time of rapid and continual technological advancements, no one is immune to the need to repurpose, reinvent, and reset their lives and their businesses. She maintains that the most essential element to facilitate all these transformations is thoughtful, clear, and cohesive communication, and she will happily step onto any available soapbox to say so.

Experienced in private, corporate, and educational environments, Rosemarie is a certified speaking coach, an internationally sought-after speaker, and founder of Confident Stages Executive Development. A 3x international best-selling author, she has championed countless individuals to reach their leadership potential by guiding them to understand how to communicate to achieve desired results and to do so with skill, presence, and finesse.

Rosemarie has presented in classrooms, boardrooms, lecture halls, theatres, and often to herself in the bathroom shower.

https://www.confidentstages.com
www.facebook.com/confidentstages/
ca.linkedin.com/in/rosemarie-barnes
@confidentstages

FROM MILITARY COMMAND TO EMPOWERED INFLUENCE: ONE WOMAN'S JOURNEY TO LEADERSHIP
BY LINDA PATTEN

From the moment I stepped on base to start my Women's Army Corps Officer Basic Training to the day I retired as a Major many years later, **I was trained to be an expert in COMMAND.** I knew how to use my command voice, how to use the preparatory command to get someone's attention, and then the command itself. I knew how to pitch my voice "just so" to get maximum volume and attention. I truly could be heard across a parade field.

I was not schooled in being collaborative, vulnerable, or in seeking consensus. I know now that the expertise I learned was the masculine model of leadership with command at its core.

Command does have its place. It has worked for men for a millennium or more. How else could you get a band of farmers and career soldiers working side-by-side to actually succeed in taking the castle? When you are in the trenches, in life-or-death situations, you need people to listen up and do what they are told. This is not a time for spirited discussion!

As General George S. Patten said, "*No good decision was ever made in a swivel chair.*" Now, this may be true on the battlefield. However, **there** *is no heart in command.* Command does not move someone to shift their opinion, take action or make change because they are inspired and believe in the cause. In fact, I say that *many* good decisions can be made in a swivel chair, or rather, many swivel chairs around a table with a lively exchange of ideas, beliefs, creativity, respectful disagreement, and passion.

INFLUENCE is a very different kind of leadership from command. "Persuasion skills exert a far greater influence over others' behaviors than formal power structures do," says Robert Cialdini, author of *Influence: The Psychology of Persuasion.* Leaders who encourage, empower, and guide their teams have a much better chance to make lasting decisions and sustainable change.

For any woman with a vision to bring change to the world – whether she's running a socially-conscious business, an arts program in the schools, a campaign for political office, or her own home – **the distinction between command and influence is an important one.**

When you use your influential leadership, you begin to change the very fabric of your world for the better. You bring people in; they willingly come along on your journey, and you are joined together in the same passion, motivation, and vision, which is a powerful formula for sustained success. Like making a patchwork quilt, each piece contributes to create one beautiful, lasting whole.

"A tiger doesn't lose sleep over the opinion of the sheep."

When I started my career in the corporate arena, I found that men in leadership roles were very much like those in the military – telling me what to do, how to do it, and expecting me to just follow along. I was such a good student of command that I didn't know there was a different way of leading or influencing. While I didn't always comply without discussion or questions, I did learn my lessons well. In turn, in my position as VP of Banking I often used my command voice with my people to "get the job done."

Not surprisingly, I had a difficult time understanding why my team and I were never close. We had a more formal relationship like I had had with my troops in the military. And I was soon to learn another twist to this whole leadership thing.

I was one of very few women in a leadership position, and the male-dominated corporate world wasn't quite used to women leaders yet. We were expected to "fit in" to that world, to be at least as competent as the men, and to hold our own in any situation. But...if we mimicked our male models' command style, they became very confused. This was not how women were supposed to act – too harsh, too aggressive, too masculine!

Even more disturbing was that the women we were "leading" were also confused and didn't like our style one bit (She's so "bossy!"). Some were heard to remark, "I don't want to be THAT leader!" When a man acted commanding, focused, decisive, fearless, it was seen as a plus. When a woman did...not so much.

Once I was even fired, despite the excellent work I produced! My boss told me there were two reasons: 1) He could never get ahold of me (I had a solution for that as I was in my car traveling for work most of the time: I suggested he get me a car phone); and 2) I was a mother and should be with my children and not working. In other words, I did not fit his model of a woman leader (What possible solution could I offer for that?).

You might remember, or have heard about, the "baking cookies" quote that Hillary Clinton made back in 1992, in response to questions as to why she was deciding to practice law while her husband was governor of Arkansas. "I suppose I could have stayed home and baked cookies and had teas, but what I decided to do was fulfill my profession, which I entered before my husband was in public life." It drew impassioned criticism from traditionalists who interpreted it as a dismissal of stay-at-home moms. But Hillary had gone on to explain that her work has been aimed at ensuring women can make choices about their personal and professional lives, "whether it's full-time career, full-time motherhood or some combination."

Footnote: In 2016, when Beyoncé performed at a rally for Hillary Clinton, she highlighted the quote on a giant screen behind her on stage. Beyoncé said, "I want my daughter to grow up seeing a woman lead our country and know that her possibilities are limitless."

When one door closes, another door opens...on Planet Entrepreneur

Back to my journey... Having been given the perfect reason to move out of corporate, I entered a new world which I like to call "Planet Entrepreneur" — a different world for sure. No more were people jumping up at attention, devoted to my command, and getting things done ASAP! The familiar rank and rules no longer applied. My team was independent women, pursuing their own goals, in their own offices or homes, managing their own time and careers and futures.

I began to observe the feminine aspect of leadership and influence. However, it wasn't until most of my team had moved away from me — abandoned me — and my clients finished their contracts without renewing that I realized I needed a different leadership mindset and model.

And what a great model it has become! I discovered that command is not true leadership. I learned that people have their own dreams, visions and goals, and that I could empower them to follow those dreams for themselves, rather than "command" them to follow mine without question. We worked together for our similar visions to blend, so all our dreams could come true. I learned that this kind of compassion, openness, vulnerability, earnest empowerment, and guidance is the kind of leadership that brings people in, energized and excited to move on their success journey together.

As Bill Gates, Founder of Microsoft, said in the '90s: "As we look ahead into the next century, leaders will be those who empower others." In today's world, true leadership has little to do with hierarchy, supreme authority, or command. Leadership is more about investing in people and trusting that they have the skills to do the work and about collaborating with others to accomplish common goals. ***There is an art and a science to these skills, and they can be learned.***

Embracing feminine leadership and influence

As I began to practice this new type of leadership, I learned that the way to invest and trust in my team was to get to know them — really get to know them (you might imagine that this was NOT the way it was done in the military). This meant getting curious, asking questions, taking a sincere interest in who they were, what was important to them, and what they uniquely bring to the table; actively seeking their ideas and opinions, inviting collaboration, and not being afraid to develop deep relationships. This meant tapping into my feminine qualities which never had had a place in the masculine world in which I lived and worked. And I loved it!

I learned how to listen, to provide a supportive ear for my people, about personal as well as professional issues. As a leader, we're not there to "solve" problems (that's not empowering); instead, we can be there to listen and provide positive, productive feedback. I incorporated into my organizational culture the core value of *treating my team and my clients how they wanted to be treated — not how I wanted to treat them.*

Not only did my businesses turn around, but I found my true purpose — training and supporting women in leadership. I started a new career, and went on to write a book and develop a 12-step system, both called *The Art of Herding Cats: Leading Teams of Leaders*, to train others how to become influential and extraordinary leaders as women.

The feminine side of leadership has everything to do with influence.

The core of the art and science of influential leadership is to recognize — and not hide — our feminine aspects. Bringing in the nurturing, compassionate, visionary qualities of the feminine will motivate and inspire a person to believe in your mission, to WANT to follow you, as opposed to BE COMMANDED to follow you.

When you believe in the value of something yourself, aren't you more apt to commit to action and see it through? It results not only in getting the job done but also providing a much richer experience.

The most effective, influential leaders bring together a marriage of feminine and masculine qualities – organization and creativity, competition and collaboration, assertiveness and empathy, analytical knowledge and intuitive wisdom, and so on. Both need to be integrated to be a powerful woman leader.

As a woman in business, you may be keeping your emotions bottled up inside because that is your perception of appearing professional. It's a natural thing to do — believe me, I know! We women have been receiving that message for a long, long time. However, your team and your clients need to see you being real. They benefit from seeing all of you, in all your quirks and imperfections as well as your most stellar talents and traits.

If you are someone whose experience is in the military or corporate world, or if you have buried your feminine leadership qualities a little too deep inside, then here are three tips to help:

Move from your head to your heart. Influence comes from the heart, command from the head. You need both, of course, to be an effective leader. But too often we are so used to the traditional masculine model that we keep on analyzing and "doing" when what we need in those moments is to tap into our heart — emotions, feelings, intuition, kindness, big picture, broad and nuanced perspective.

Embrace your feminine side. Go ahead, don't be afraid! Your masculine side is still there, available when you need it; you are not weak because you embrace your feminine! Welcome it into your relationships, make magic with it! Allow yourself to be curious, to ask questions, to collaborate, cooperate, show empathy and compassion, be patient, share yourself openly.

Recognize that the masculine side completes you but does not define you. Your masculine side is important: freedom, direction, focus, integrity, independence, confidence, action, and, yes, assertiveness. When you recognize and invite in your full self — masculine and feminine — you can see from these qualities I've listed how influential and powerful that combination can make you!

Is your leadership style more masculine or feminine? How can you be more balanced?

In a program out of Wharton University, called "Women in Leadership: Legacies, Opportunities and Challenges," women in business and influence are encouraged to be "exceptionally aware" of their own leadership styles and strengths in order to make an impact. They want us to continually "build our strengths and skills so we can lead a variety of people," especially because the feminine includes that capacity for empathy. They advise us to also be aware of and develop our masculine capabilities so that we can become more effective and powerful leaders.

At the same time, we are taking part in changing old perceptions of what a leader is or should be, of changing that dynamic for our generation and for generations of women to come.

I'm grateful for my journey, my experience of seeing the more extreme aspects of leadership in action — in the military and in the corporate world during a period when women were just coming into their true power (and of course we are still on that journey). What I know today is that leadership exists on a spectrum — there are masculine and feminine ways to lead and to influence. One end of the spectrum isn't better than the other.

In fact, **the best leaders are those who marry the two into one unique, empowered extraordinary leader!**

This "marriage" comes into play in my work, especially with creative entrepreneurs who tend to be more comfortable in their feminine aspect so are challenged by their relationships with time, money, and planning (masculine, left-brain side). Skills like organization, structure, and strategy are not in their wheelhouse – but they are in mine! My genius is in these more masculine aspects. When we work together, we tap into, integrate, and leverage our masculine AND feminine qualities to become truly powerful, comfluential™ leaders.

My hope and vision for you and for all the women I work with is to honor YOUR unique brand of leadership, your own way of influencing others, tapping into all your natural feminine instincts to express your emotions, along with your natural masculine abilities to focus, get tasks done, and make confident decisions. Learning about and bringing out all of these amazing qualities — and the results you can see in making change — is an exciting and lifelong journey.

Bon voyage, Woman of Impassioned Influence and Fearless Leadership!

Linda Patten

Linda Patten is founder of *Dare2Lead with Linda*, international speaker and best-selling author, talk radio show host on the VoiceAmerica Empowerment Channel, leadership expert, and trainer. Her life's work is challenging women to dare to lead: whether it is for navigating the often-daunting entrepreneurial world, building strong teams for a thriving business, stepping out of the shadows into the light as a leader of one's life, or learning the leadership skills that will grow the seeds of change into a world-level movement.

With 40 years of leadership experience spanning the military (including protocol officer to a 4-star general), corporate, and entrepreneurial arenas, Linda is uniquely qualified to guide women on their journey of self-discovery, skills development, and a charted course toward becoming an extraordinary leader. Her book and 12-step program, *The Art of Herding Cats: Leading Teams of Leaders*, are rooted in her heartfelt vision to empower women to step out, step up, and step into the kind of leadership that creates positive change in the world.

Linda is a gifted communicator who is regularly featured live and online on business panels, interviewed as a leadership expert, and as a popular speaker and seminar leader on topics related to women in business and leadership. She holds an MBA in Organizational Behavior and Leadership, a Certificate in Meeting Management, as well as leadership positions in numerous professional management associations and women's business networking groups.

Email Address: linda@dare2leadwithlinda.com
Phone Number: 925-954-3239
Website: www.dare2leadwithlinda.com
Facebook page(s): https://www.facebook.com/dare2leadwithlinda; https://www.facebook.com/linda.patten.311
Linked In: https://www.linkedin.com/in/lindapatten
Twitter Handle: @patten_linda
You Tube Channel: http://www.youtube.com/c/LindaPatten
Other Social Media Channels:
https://plus.google.com/+LindaPatten
https://www.pinterest.com/lindapatten311/

Closing Thoughts

I hope you have been touched by these powerful chapters that have encouraged, equipped, and empowered you to live on purpose while shining powerfully in your own style of leadership! We hope you have been encouraged on your leadership journey and are inspired to apply the practical and profound tips, advice, and great wisdom into your life. We can't wait to see you, hear from you, and celebrate you as you share the gift of you with the world! May you always choose to **live on purpose and with great purpose.**

****

Books compiled or written by Rebecca Hall Gruyter to be released in 2019 and 2020:

Step Into Your Brilliance!

This anthology featuring up to 20 authors (the first book in the *Step Into* anthology series) will empower readers to discover and embrace their brilliance. This book will then equip and empower the reader to share their own brilliance with the world. The world needs you and your brilliance! (To be released in September of 2019.)

The Animal Legacies!

This anthology featuring up to 20 authors will share heart-warming, inspiring, empowering true stories of how animals have powerfully touched their lives. They will share a profound lesson they learned, a powerful truth, a powerful legacy, encouraging messages, a celebration

172 | EXPERTS & INFLUENCERS

and honor of our animal friends. Every reader will be encouraged and their heart touched as each writer shares and passes to you their own animal legacy. We know this book will touch your heart and life. (To be released December 2019).

The Expert and Influencers Series: Women's Empowerment Edition

This powerful anthology will feature up to 30 experts and influencers committed to empowering you in the area of Women's Empowerment. They will share tips, advice, and powerful insight to help you step forward as a leader in your life and business. (To be released June 2020.)

Step Into Your Mission and Purpose!

This anthology featuring up to 30 authors (the second book in the *Step Into* anthology series) will empower readers to discover and embrace their brilliance. This book will then equip and empower the reader to discover their mission and purpose so that they can live each day on purpose and with great purpose. The world needs you and your brilliance! (To be released in September of 2020).

Anthologies Available Now That Are Compiled by Rebecca Hall Gruyter:

SHINE Series (Compiled and led by Rebecca Hall Gruyter)
    Come out of Hiding and SHINE! (Book 1)
    Bloom Where You are Planted and SHINE! (Book 2)
    Step Forward and SHINE! (Book 3)

Step Into Series (Compiled and led by Rebecca Hall Gruyter)
    Step Into Your Brilliance! (Book 1)
    Step Into Your Mission & Purpose! (Book 2)

Experts & Influencers Series (Compiled and led by Rebecca Hall Gruyter)
    Experts & Influencers Series: Leadership (Book 1)

Experts & Influencers Series: Women's Empowerment (Book 2)

The Grandmother Legacies (Anthology Compiled by Rebecca Hall Gruyter)

Empowering YOU, Transforming Lives (365 Daily Inspiration Anthology Compiled by Rebecca Hall Gruyter)

Books Available Now Featuring a Chapter by Rebecca Hall Gruyter:

The 40/40 Rules, Anthology compiled by Holly Porter
Becoming Outrageously Successful, Anthology compiled by Dr. Anita Jackson
Catch Your Star, Anthology published by THRIVE Publishing
Discover Your Destiny, Anthology compiled by Denise Joy Thompson
I Am Beautiful, Anthology compiled by Teresa Hawley-Howard
The Power of Our Voices, Sharing Our Story, Anthology compiled by Teresa Hawley-Howard
Succeeding Against All Odds, Anthology compiled by Sandra Yancey
Success Secrets for Today's Feminine Entrepreneurs, Anthology compiled by Dr. Anita Jackson
Unstoppable Woman of Purpose, Anthology and workbook, compiled by Nella Chikwe
Women on a Mission, Anthology compiled by Teresa Hawley-Howard
Women of Courage, Women of Destiny, Anthology compiled by Dr. Anita Jackson
Women Warriors Who Make It Rock, Anthology compiled by Nichole Peters
You Are Whole, Perfect, and Complete - Just As You Are compiled by Carol Plummer and Susan Driscoll

****

Dear Powerful Reader,

Thank you for reading our anthology. I hope it has encouraged and empowered you and uplifted you in the area of leadership.

I wanted to share a little bit more about our organizations, Your Purpose Driven Practice™, RHG TV Network™, RHG Publishing™ and RHG Media Productions™. We are passionate about helping others live on purpose and with purpose in their life and business. I hope this book has supported and inspired you to choose to live on purpose and with great purpose in your leadership!

If you are wanting to reach more people and be part of inspiring and supporting others with your message, your gifts, and the work that you bring to the world, then I want to share some opportunities for you to consider.

Each year we compile and produce anthology book projects, support authors in publishing their own powerful books as best sellers, produce and publish an international magazine, launch TV shows, facilitate women's empowerment conferences, get quoted in major media, launch radio and podcast shows, and help experts and speakers step into a place of powerful influence to make a global difference. We provide programs and strategies to help you reach more people, and facilitate the Speaker Talent Search (which helps speakers, experts, and influencers connect with more speaking opportunities). We would love to support you in reaching more people. Please take a moment to learn a little bit more about us at the sites listed below, and then reach out to us for a conversation. **We would love to help you be Seen, Heard, and SHINE!**

You can learn more about each of these things on our main website: www.YourPurposeDrivenPractice.com

Enjoy our powerful **TV and podcast shows**: www.RHGTVNetwork.com

Learn more about the **Speaker Talent Search™**: www.Speaker TalentSearch.com

Learn more about our **writing opportunities**: http://yourpurpose drivenpractice.com/writing-opportunities/

If you would like to connect with me personally to explore some of our opportunities in upcoming book projects, podcast/radio shows, and/or TV, then here is the link to schedule a time to speak with me directly: www.MeetWithRebecca.com or you can email me at: Rebecca@YourPuposeDrivenPractice.com

May you always choose to Be Seen, Heard and SHINE!

Warmly,

Rebecca Hall Gruyter